DIARY OF A TAR HEEL CONFEDERATE SOLDIER

by
Louis Leon

THE CONFEDERATE
REPRINT COMPANY
☆   ☆   ☆   ☆
WWW.CONFEDERATEREPRINT.COM

Diary of a Tar Heel Confederate Soldier
by Louis Leon

Originally Published in 1913
by Stone Publishing Company
Charlotte, North Carolina

Reprint Edition © 2014
The Confederate Reprint Company
Post Office Box 2027
Toccoa, Georgia 30577
www.confederatereprint.com

Cover and Interior Design by
Magnolia Graphic Design
www.magnoliagraphicdesign.com

ISBN-13: 978-0692288214
ISBN-10: 069228821X

Louis Leon

PREFACE

This diary was commenced for the fun of writing down my experience as a soldier from the Old North State. I never thought for a moment that I would put it in print; but now that I am getting old and have read so many histories written by our officers, I have never seen in print a history written by a private.

I know that my diary is truly the life of the man behind the gun, therefore I make bold to publish it. I am sure my experience was that of other privates, and a true history of my companies and regiments, as well as the Brigade, Division, and even Corp that I belonged to. I am certain that the men of '61 to '65 who read this will recall most vividly the camping, marching, fighting and suffering they endured in those never-to-be-forgotten days of long ago. And to the younger generation of Southern-born it will show how we endured and suffered, but still fought on for the cause we know was right.

L. Leon

CHAPTER ONE
The Beginning

April 25, 1861 — I belong to the Charlotte Grays, Company C, First North Carolina Regiment. We left home for Raleigh. Our company is commanded by Capt. Egbert Ross. We are all boys between the ages of eighteen and twenty-one. We offered our services to Governor Ellis, but were afraid he would not take us, as we are so young; but before we were called out our company was ordered to go to the United States Mint in our town and take same. We marched down to it, and it was surrendered to us. We guarded it several days, when we were ordered to Raleigh, and left on the above date.

Our trip was full of joy and pleasure, for at every station where our train stopped the ladies showered us with flowers and Godspeed. We marched to the Fair Grounds. The streets were lined with people, cheering us. When we got there our company was given quarters, and, lo and behold! horse stables with straw for bedding is what we got. I know we all thought it a disgrace for us to sleep in such places with our fine uniforms — not even a washstand, or any place to hang our clothes on. They didn't even give us a looking-glass.

Our company was put in the First North Carolina Regiment, commanded by Col. D.H. Hill, Lieut.-Col. C. C. Lee, and Maj. James H. Lane.

We enlisted for six months. Our State went out of the Union on May 20th, and we were sent to Richmond, Va., on the 21st. Stayed there several days, when we were ordered to Yorktown, Va. Here they gave us tents to sleep in. This looked more like soldiering, but we would have liked to have had some of that straw in Raleigh.

The day after we got here our company was sent out with spades and shovels to make breastworks — and to think of the indignity! We were expected to do the digging! Why, of course, I never thought that this was work for soldiers to do, but we had to do it. Gee! What hands I had after a few days' work. I know I never had a pick or a shovel in my hand to work with in my life.

A few days after that a squad of us were sent out to cut down trees, and, by George! they gave me an axe and told me to go to work. Well, I cut all over my tree until the lieutenant commanding, seeing how nice I was marking it, asked me what I had done before I became a soldier. I told him I was a clerk in a dry-goods store. He said he thought so from the way I was cutting timber. He relieved me — but what insults are put on us who came to fight the Yankees! Why, he gave me two buckets and told me to carry water to the men that could cut.

We changed camp several times, until about the 3d of June, when we marched fifteen miles and halted at Bethel Church, and again commenced making breastworks. Our rations did not suit us. We wanted a change of diet, but there were strict orders from Col. D.H. Hill that we should not go out foraging. Well, Bill Stone, Alie Todd and myself put on our knapsacks and went to the creek to wash our clothes, but when we got there we forgot to wash. We took a good long walk away from the camp, and saw several shoats. We ran one down, held it so it could not squeal, then killed it, cut it in small pieces, put it in our knapsacks, returned to the creek, and from there to camp, where we shared it with the boys. It tasted good.

Our comrade Ernheart did not fare so well. He went to a place where he knew he could get some honey. He got it all right, but he got the bees, also. His face and hands were a sight when he got the beehive to camp.

June 10 — At three o'clock this morning the long roll woke us up. We fell in line, marched about five miles, then counter-marched, as the Yankees were advancing on us. We got to our breastworks a short time before the Yankees came, and firing commenced. We gave them a good reception with shot and shell. The fight lasted about four hours. Our company was behind the works that held the line where the major of the Yankee regiment, Winthrop, was killed. After he fell our company was ordered to the church, but was soon sent back to its former position.

This is the first land battle of the war, and we certainly gave them a good beating, but we lost one of our regiment, Henry Wyatt, who was killed while gallantly doing a volunteer duty. Seven of our men were wounded. The Yankees must have lost at least two hundred men in killed and wounded. It was their boast that they could whip us with corn-stalks, but to their sorrow they found that we could do some fighting, too. After the fight some of the boys and myself went over the battlefield, and we saw several of the Yankee dead — the first I had ever seen, and it made me shudder. I am now in a school where sights like this should not worry me long.

Our commander in this fight was Col. Bankhead Magruder. The Yankee commander was Gen. B.F. Butler.

From now on I will never again grumble about digging breastworks. If it had not been for them many of us would not be here now. We returned the same night to Yorktown, full of glory.

On July 18 we heard that our boys had again whipped the Yankees at Bull Run.

Also, on July 21, again at Manassas.

We changed camp a number of times, made fortifications all around Yorktown, and when our six months were over we were disbanded, and returned home. So my experience as a soldier was over.

I stayed home five months, when I again took arms for the Old North State, and joined a company raised by Capt. Harvey White, of Charlotte, and left our home on April 23, 1862, at 6.30 P.M. I stayed in Salisbury until next night, when I, with several others, took the train for Raleigh, where our company was. We went to the insane asylum to see Langfreid, who wanted to go home by telegraph to see his cotton and tobacco. After spending most of our day in town we went to camp four miles from Raleigh. We stopped a carriage, and the driver said he would take us to camp for three dollars. We halved it with him and he drove us there. We reported to Captain White, and he showed us to our hut. We were surprised to find it without a floor, roof half off and "holey" all over. We commenced repairing, and went to the woods to chop a pole for a part of the bedstead. We walked about a mile before we found one to suit us. It was a hard job to get it to our hut. We put it up and put boards across and then put our bedding on it, which consisted of leaves we gathered in the woods. And now it is a bed fit for a king or a Confederate soldier.

It commenced raining at dark, which compelled us to cover with our oilcloth coats. We did not get wet, but passed a bad night, as I had gotten used to a civilian's life again.

May 31 — Up to date nothing transpired worth relating, but this morning got orders to leave. Left at 6 A.M. Our company got passenger cars, and the balance of our regiment had to take box cars.

June 1 — Arrived at Weldon, North Carolina, at 7 o'clock. We set up our tents at Gerresburg, a short march from Weldon. Our company is close to the railroad track. We collected broom straw and made a bed of down of it.

June 2 — We received some visitors from home.

June 3 — Raining all day, but have a good time with the ladies in this neighborhood. They treated my comrade and myself only as Southern ladies know how to treat their soldiers — with respect and something good to eat.

June 4 — Still raining, and the roads are very muddy.

June 5 — We were marched to town and received our arms — Springfield muskets. Next day went off very quietly.

June 7 — At 11 o'clock to-night we were roused out of our sleep and marched to Weldon Bridge, as the river was so swift that it was thought the bridge would wash away. We went there to knock the sides off, so that the water could run over it, but we got there without tools. When they came the water was receding, so we returned to camp.

June 8 — I am very tired from our first night's march.

June 20 — Up until this date there has been nothing worth recording, but to-day got orders to fall in line with two days' rations cooked. Left at 12 M. in box cars. We knocked holes in them to get fresh air. We laid over six hours eight miles from Gerresburg in order to let the passenger cars pass us. Several of our company left the train in quest of supper. We found a house where a lady promised to give us supper for fifty cents each. As we were doing full justice to her supper the train started, we left in a hurry, and did not have time to pay for our meal. I don't suppose she gave us her blessing.

June 21 — We reached Petersburg, Va., this morning at half-past two, and had barely laid down with a brick wall for my pillow when breakfast was announced in the shape of Mack Sample, who told us where we could get it. I ran the blockade with Katz, and went to see Mike Etlinger. He was not at home. Afterward we met Wortheim, and we all went again and got something good to eat. We then returned to our regiment, which is the 53d North Carolina Regiment, infantry, Col. William Owens, commander. We are enlisted for three years, or the war. We fell in line and marched to our camp, which is on Dunn's Hill, just outside of the city.

June 22 — Nothing new.

June 23 — Moved our camp two miles up the road toward Richmond. It is a very bad camp — low ground and muddy. But there is a factory here, and plenty of girls to make up for the damp ground.

June 24 — We had a drill to-day, and went to town to see some friends.

June 25 — Reported fighting near Richmond.

June 26 — We received marching orders this morning. The long roll beat at one in the night. We marched four miles on to Richmond, where we met some wounded of our army that had been injured at the Point of Rocks. We got to this place after marching all night, too late for the Yanks — they had gone. We stayed here until the 28th, then marched to Drewry's Bluff, twenty miles from Petersburg.

June 29 — Arrived at Drewry's Bluff this morning. Here we met our brigade, commanded by General Daniels. The brigade has five regiments, all North Carolina troops, composed of the 43d, 53d, 32d, 45th and the 2d North Carolina battalions. When we got to our brigade we were left at Drewry's Bluff and the brigade marched on to Richmond, and we stayed here until the 30th.

June 30 — Heard firing at Richmond. We are eight miles from there, and in reserve.

July 1 — There is nothing new, only we can see the lines of battle over the river. They are still fighting around Richmond.

July 4 — This is the day the Yankee general, McClellan, promised to eat dinner in our capitol. He did not, but numbers of his command did — that is, in our prisons. But they did not get any turkey.

July 6 — We got orders to march this morning. Left here with two days' rations of corn meal and bacon in our haversacks. We got to Petersburg in the evening — fifteen miles — after a hard march. It is very warm, and we did not rest on the way, as it was a forced march. We camped on Dunn's Hill.

July 7 — We return to our factory girls again — all O.K., you bet.

July 27 — Had a few friends visit us from home,

and moved camp twice. To-night we were ordered to fall in line. Went to Petersburg, and there took the cars for Weldon. On the road a dreadful accident occurred. On the flat car that we were on, a captain of the navy with us had his leg cut off by a sheet of iron flying off the flat. Lieutenant McMatthews, Henry Wortheim and myself were knocked down, but not badly hurt. The captain died two days after.

July 31 — Up to this time there is nothing new. We are camped at Weldon.

August 1 — From date to the 4th — nothing. We have a good camp.

August 5 — We received marching orders to-day. We embarked on the train at Weldon, went down the Seaboard road a distance of twenty-five miles, and marched from there to Roberts' Chapel. Our company and Company D were the only ones that went. We got there at 10 o'clock at night and laid in the woods until morning.

August 6 — We fell in line and returned. We marched to Boykins and took the cars to our regiment again. This expedition was to capture Yankees that are stealing negroes. When we got there they had left.

Up to August 19 — Nothing new. We have a very good time here by ourselves — get plenty to eat from the ladies and visit them whenever we can get out of camp.

August 20 — Left here at 6 P.M. and arrived at Petersburg at 3 o'clock in the morning. Took the same bed that I had the last time — the sidewalk — and the wall for my pillow. Katz, Hugh Sample, "Bat" Harry, Lieutenant Belk and some others were left behind, sick.

August 21 — Left at 4 A.M. and arrived in Richmond at 6 P.M. Marched to Camp Lee, two miles from the city, and put up any tent we could get hold of, as it was raining very hard and too dark to see. We are all O.K. now.

August 22 — Sam Oppenheim, of the 44th North Carolina Regiment, an old comrade of the 1st North Carolina Regiment, came to see me. He is stationed on the other side of the city.

August 23 — Went uptown to see my brother, Morris, of the 44th Georgia Regiment; but his regiment had already gone to Gordonsville, so I returned to camp.

August 26 — Up to date did not get half enough to eat.

August 27 — Three of our companies got Enfield rifles to-day.

August 28 — Ordered to Drewry's Bluff. We left Richmond at 8 P.M. and got there at 2 A.M. We are camping on the old oat patch, near our former camp.

August 29 — Lieutenant Belk, whom we left at Weldon, sick, returned to us to-day.

August 30 — Our company went to work to-day throwing up breastworks.

August 31 — Still digging dirt.

September 1 — Wortheim and myself went to Half-way Station, to get a box that was sent to us from home, but it did not come.

September 9 — Up to to-day nothing new. Our regiment was paid off to-day, we receiving one month's wages — eleven dollars for a private, which I have the honor to be.

September 18 — Nothing new, only plenty of bad weather and hard work. We received marching orders at 9 A.M. We arrived in Petersburg at 5 P.M. Saw several friends there. Left Petersburg at 8 o'clock that night in cars for Wakefield. Arrived there at 11 A.M.

September 19 — Left Wakefield at 9 P.M. and

marched twenty miles — laid in the woods without shelter and it raining very hard. Therefore did not need to wash myself in the morning.

September 20 — Resumed our march at 6 o'clock this morning. Arrived at Blacks Church after three hours' march, then turned about and tramped nine miles and camped for the night at Joyner's Church.

September 21 — Left here at 6 P.M., marched nine miles, and halted for dinner. Our company being rear guard of the brigade, we had a hard time of it, as the roads are very muddy and we had to keep up all the stragglers. We reached Wakefield at 5 A.M., and laid in the woods and mud for the night.

September 22 — We laid here all day. Cars came for us from Petersburg to-night and took us back. Got there at 12 at night, marched one mile and camped for the night.

September 23 — Left here this morning at 10 o'clock and got to our old camp at 4 o'clock this evening. This expedition was to strengthen Longstreet's forces near Suffolk. We got there after he was relieved and the siege of Suffolk abandoned.

September 27 — Up to to-day nothing new, only today is my New Year (the Jewish New Year).

October — This month passed off with nothing new, except Katz returned on the 7th, and Donau was discharged. We are still on our old camp.

November 5 — There is nothing for me to write. To-day Wortheim and myself went to Petersburg to get a box that was sent from home, and while there we had a very good time.

November 6 — We commenced to put up winter quarters to-day. It is very cold and sleeting.

November 7 — It commenced to snow this morning at 6 o'clock, and continued until one in the afternoon. It is three inches deep. We got some whiskey into camp, which tasted very good and made us forget the cold. The balance of this month passed off very quietly. We are hard at work on our winter huts.

December 1 and 2 — We moved into our winter quarters. They are very good and strong. There are ten men in each hut.

December 3 — Katz and myself went to Petersburg to-day. We met with friends, and the consequence you can imagine. The headache we had next day was caused by too much whiskey.

December 8 — My birthday to-day. I am a man twenty-one years old, but I must say that I have been doing a man's duty before I was twenty-one, providing a soldier's duty is a man's. I spent to-day in bringing mud to our palace for a fireplace.

December 13 — There was nothing to record up to the 13th, but to-day had division review from 9 A.M. until 5 P.M.

December 14 — Rumored that we will leave Virginia for North Carolina.

December 15 — Sure enough. Got orders to cook five days' rations. We started at 2 A.M. and got to Petersburg at 8 o'clock that night. I ran the blockade, and went uptown and stayed all night and had a very good time.

December 16 — I returned this morning and was not missed. We left here with the cars at 8 A.M., and got to Weldon at 3 P.M. on the 17th.

December 17 — Laid in an old field until 8 P.M., and suffered a great deal from cold. We left here on flat cars and rode all night on them. We arrived at Goldsboro at 10 A.M. on the 18th. The ladies on the road, especially those at Wilson, were very kind to us. They gave us plenty to eat, which we were very much in need of.

December 18 — We marched through town and lay all night in an open field without tents. It is certainly bitter cold. The only fires we could make were from the fence rails, as the woods were too far for us to get to.

December 19 — We got away from the open field at 12 M., and went two miles out of town, and camped in the woods. We met the Bethel regiment to-day. I met quite a number of old friends and comrades of my old company. We compared notes on soldiering. We came to the conclusion that at Yorktown we were playing soldier, but now there is no play in it. We are expecting a fight every hour.

December 20 — Went uptown to-day on French leave, and when I returned was put on guard duty for going.

December 21 — I went to the creek to wash my clothing and myself, and when I got back the water had frozen on my head so that I was obliged to hold my head by the fire so as to thaw it out. Wortheim's eyes are so bad that he can hardly see. Sam Wilson broke his shoulder blade.

December 25 — There is nothing new up to to-day, Christmas. We moved our camp a little piece. Eigenbrun came to see us to-day from home, and brought me a splendid cake from Miss Clara Phile. This is certainly a hard Christmas for us — bitter cold, raining and snowing all the time, and we have no tents. The only shelter we have is a blanket spread over a few poles, and gather leaves and put them in that shelter for a bed.

December 26 — I got vaccinated to-day by Capt.

Harvey White. It was raining very hard, and we all are as wet as dish rags.

December 31 — All is quiet up to to-day, the last of the year. It is still very cold.

CHAPTER TWO
The Year 1863

January 1 — This month we have done nothing but move our camp once, and drill. Had to send all our baggage away. Hereafter nothing more will be hauled for us in wagons. There are rumors flying about that we will soon leave here.

February 1 and 2 — There is nothing new, but cold, cold, cold.

February 4 — This morning, at 4 o'clock, we were waked up by the pleasant sound of long roll. We were ordered to get ready to march. It is very cold, snow nine inches deep. We laid in Goldsboro until noon, expecting to get cars to take us away, but were then told we would have to march to Kinston. We took up our line of march at 3 in the evening and halted at dark. It is truly awful. The snow is very deep and as cold as thunder. We marched eight miles without resting. We then fixed our bed in the snow and stole fodder for a bed and rails to make fire. We took snow, put it in our kettles, and made coffee. When I say coffee, I mean Confederate coffee — parched corn —

that is our coffee. Ate our corn bread and bacon and retired to our couches and slept as good if not better than Abe Lincoln.

February 5 — Resumed our promenade at 7 this morning, and for a change it is raining hard. Therefore the snow is melting. Consequently, the roads are nice and soft. Halted at 3 this evening — still raining. We made ourselves as comfortable as possible — made a good fire to dry ourselves by, but the worst of it is we have no rations, and the wagons are behind. We went to sleep in our wet clothing, with a cup of coffee as our supper. It rained and snowed all night.

February 6 — Nothing to eat yet. Wortheim, W. Eagle and myself went out foraging, to buy something to eat. We got to one house and there was no one at home, but in the yard there were two chickens, which we captured, for we were afraid they would bite us. We went to the next house and ate our breakfast. One of the ladies asked us where we got those chickens. I told her that we bought them at the house before we got there. She told us she lived there and that there was nobody at home. I then told her the truth, paid her for them and left. The next house we got to we bought a ham, a peck of meal, a peck of sweet potatoes and some turnips. We took dinner in this house. We then returned to camp. We had a good reception from our mess, as they had still nothing to eat.

February 7 — We could not march yesterday, as the streams were too high from the recent rains and snow. We left to-day at 12 M., and got one day's rations, hard enough to fell a bull. Marched on the railroad track all the afternoon. The main road was impassable. We got to Kinston at 4 in the afternoon, and made camp in a swamp, two and a half miles out of town. We had nothing to eat, but slept good for all that.

February 8 — Wortheim and myself went uptown to get something to eat. We got corn bread and bacon. On our road back to camp we bought four more dodgers of corn bread and gave it to our mess companions who did not go uptown. Our regiment moved on the other side of town in an old pine thicket.

February 9 — We established a regular camp here. This last march has been a very hard one, and only a distance of thirty miles. But it took us from Wednesday to Saturday, through snow, rain and mud ankle-deep and without rations. Kinston is a perfect ruin, as the Yankees have destroyed everything they could barely touch, but it must at one time have been a very pretty town — but now nothing scarcely but chimneys are left to show how the Yankees are trying to reconstruct the Union.

February 13 — Nothing new. We have been fixing our camps. Our company has built log huts, from two to three feet high, and then put our tents over them — building a chimney to each hut or tent, and we are very comfortable. We got orders to cook two days' rations, and be ready to march in two hours, but did not have to go — in fact, nothing new until the 25th.

February 25 — Henry Wortheim was sent home on a sick furlough, as he is very bad off.

February 26 — Two men out of our regiment were whipped for desertion. They were undressed all but pants and shoes, tied to a post, and each given thirty-nine lashes on their bare backs. The balance of this month nothing new, only very cold.

March 5 — Up to to-day there is nothing worth recording, although we are getting black as negroes on account of our burning green pine.

March 6 — Several of us out of our company went to Kinston and the battlefield. The Yankees are very poorly buried, as we saw several heads, hands and feet sticking out of the ground, where the rain had washed the dirt off of them.

March 12 — We have had orders several times for the last six days to march, and a part of our brigade has had a fight. But this morning we took up our march at 5 o'clock. I saw Gen. D. H. Hill on the road and spoke to him, as well as his adjutant. They are friends from home and comrades of our first North Carolina regiment. We marched twenty miles and halted for the night — laid in line of battle all night with arms by our side.

March 13 — Resumed our march at 8 this morning, got eight miles, when we got to our extreme picket posts. They told us the Yankees were one mile and a quarter from us. Then we marched half a mile further, when our artillery commenced the fight. It kept on all day, but very light. We drove in their pickets and advanced our line until dark. We are eight miles from Newbern — marched eleven miles.

March 14 — This morning, at daybreak, cannonading was heard by us from General Pettigrew's line, which is on our left flank. We immediately fell into line of battle, our artillery opened fire, then we infantry advanced our line on the Yankees. We halted in an old field and had for a breastwork a rail fence. We fought for four hours — hot at times. We had a number killed and wounded. The enemy fell back on their stronghold — Newbern. This battle is called the Battle of Deep Gully, as it was fought on that stream. We then took up our march again for Kinston. We got eleven miles and halted for the night. Our company was the rear guard of the brigade.

March 15 — Laid here all day, with two crackers for our rations, and these we got at night.

March 16 — A picket came in this morning and reported the enemy advancing. We were put in line of battle to receive them, and after marching one mile up the road to get to our brigade we were put at the extreme left of our line, and made breastworks out of rotten logs. Stayed here one hour, when another picket came and reported them ten miles away. So we resumed our march for camp and got there at 7 o'clock — twenty-one miles to-day. Tom Notter, Aaron Katz and myself pressed into service to-day a donkey and a cart with a negro, who took us to Kinston. Each of us drove at times, and I was fortunate enough to stall in a mudhole. We had to get out and lift the cart and donkey to dry ground again. Thus ends the march and fight at Deep Gully.

March 20 — Katz went home to-day on a furlough. Nothing new up to the 23d.

March 23 — We had a man whipped to-day in our regiment for desertion.

March 24 — Commenced marching this morning, got seventeen miles and halted. Laid here in the woods until the 27th. Went to several houses and had a good time with ladies and eatables up to the 29th.

March 29 — Here still, but positively don't know where we are.

March 30 — Left this morning at 5 o'clock, marched fifteen miles. Waded clay-bottom swamps three-quarters of a mile long. This is in Pitt County, North Carolina. We then camped in the woods and made fires to dry ourselves with.

March 31 — Left at 7 this morning, marched six miles, waded several creeks, and arrived at Swift Creek at

11. This is a small village. We camp here for the night.

April 1 — Left here on the Little Washington dirt road at 7 this morning. Marched seventeen miles and halted three miles from Washington. This is a Yankee post. Heard firing all day, and we are ordered to keep our cartridge boxes on us and our guns by our sides, as we may move any moment.

April 2 — Our regiment was sent on picket this morning at daylight — one mile from camp and two miles from the enemy. Companies B and G are on the left, A and D on the right, F and I in the center. We are within hailing distance of the Yankee line of pickets. There is not much firing. Tom Tiotter and I are on the color guard. We have nothing to do if we don't want to, except stay with the colors. So this evening at 4 o'clock we went as near the Yankees as we dared, to see the town of Washington. Saw the place, their breastworks and their camps very plainly. We then returned and slept on our arms all night — that is, we tried to sleep, but could not for the infernal noise from the owls that are in the swamps around us.

April 3 — Little Washington is on Tar River, and as one of the Yankee gunboats was trying to get in, one of our cannon gave them a ball, which caused heavy firing all day, and, in fact, the shells came very close to our flag, which made us dodge pretty smart. We have Washington besieged. At 8 o'clock to-night Colonel Owens called for volunteers to go as near the Yankees as they could, to see what they were doing. Tom Tiotter and myself went. We got to within two hundred yards of Washington, when we were compelled to halt, as we were near the bridge, where we could hear the Yankee sentinels walking their beats very plainly — so we returned to camp and reported.

April 4 — Firing at intervals all day. The reserve

was sent to the river to support our artillery. The colors went with them. It is raining hard. We laid in line two and a half hours in an old field. It is very cold. The Yankees are firing all the time. Then the 43d Regiment came and relieved us. Katz came in to-day and reported Henry Wortheim dead — he died Monday, March 30.

April 5 — Everything is quiet on our line to-day.

April 6 — A little firing to-day. Went to the river to throw up breastworks. Worked all night. We put up one piece of cannon right on the river bank, but had to work all night in the swamp to do so. We carried sandbags for breastworks to protect the artillerymen.

April 7 — To-day the firing was very heavy. We hit the Yankee gunboat again to-day, and made the dust fly out of their breastworks.

April 8 — This morning Tom Tiotter, Katz and myself went with Captain White to meet three Yankees with a flag of truce; but they would not come half way, so Colonel Owens ordered us back. We then — we three — went to our siege-gun and saw the town very plainly. They fired at us while we were there. The fire was returned, and we could see the Yankees dodge.

April 9 — We were relieved this morning by the 32d Regiment, and marched to Bellevue, where the balance of our brigade is. At 11 o'clock to-night we were ordered to march. We went fifteen miles. There was a fight there to-day. Marched all night without resting.

April 10 — Got to our line at 6 this morning. The Yankees had fallen back. They had nineteen regiments and twenty-one pieces of artillery. They left in a hurry. One of their colonels was killed and I don't know how many men. We left Blount Creek Bridge at 4 this evening, marched nine miles on our way back to Bellevue. We met the Bethel regiment, and I met several friends of my old company.

April 13 — Up to date they are firing at Fort Hill and Washington all the time.

April 14 — Nothing.

April 15 — Raining very hard. We have a blanket spread over poles to keep us dry. We got orders to march this evening. Went five miles through mud and water, and it raining like fury. I shall long remember this march, as well as a few others of my company. We fell in the mud several times, and were certainly beautiful objects to look at with our suits of mud, for we were completely covered with it.

April 16 — At 7 this morning we resumed our march. Went two miles, halted a half hour, then turned about and went to our old camp, but again were ordered back at 2 P.M. to our picket posts, one mile from Washington. As we got there the Yankees gave us a good reception in shot, shell and musketry, but all the damage they did was to rail fences and perhaps a few owls that are plentiful in the swamps. Our line is on the edge of the swamp. They shelled heavy all night, but no lives were lost on our side. At 8 P.M. our pickets fired on them, but they did not respond. We laid here until 2 at night, when we went to Bellevue under fire from the enemy. We stayed here the balance of the night.

April 17 — At daylight this morning our company was ordered to go on picket at Shingle Landing, five miles from Bellevue. I asked Colonel Morehead to let me go with them, but he refused, and said I should stay with the colors, but I went without his permission. In a march of five miles we waded through three miles of swamp, knee-deep. We are in a devil of a position. The enemy can cut us off from our command easily, as we cannot return, except through the swamp, which of course would be very slow progress. At 4 this evening we were recalled, and met our regiment on the march and fell in. Colonel Morehead did not miss me from the colors. We marched seven miles and halted for the night.

April 18 — Left at 9 this morning, and got to Greenville at 5 o'clock — eleven miles. This is a fine country, but hilly and hard marching. This is the end of the siege of Washington. We were there sixteen days, but could not draw the enemy out of their works.

April 19 — Nothing to-day but rest, which we needed very much.

April 20 — Went on picket this morning to the south side of the town, across the river, but did not go on picket. Our company and Company G supported two pieces of artillery. I was again refused permission by Morehead to go with my company, but I went all the same.

April 21 — Nothing doing.

April 22 — Ordered to our brigade at 12 M.

April 23 — Raining hard all day and night. No shelter. We got as wet as drowned cats.

April 24 — This morning I was detailed by Colonel Owens to go to Wilson, N.C., to get the baggage for our officers. Left at 3 A.M., got to Tarboro at 7 P.M. This is a very pretty town. Stayed here until 3 and took the cars to Rocky Mount. Got there at 5, left at 7, and got to Wilson at 8 on the morning of the 25th. Got my baggage and left at 3 P.M. Arrived at Rocky Mount at 4. Saw some fun with a girl and an old woman. The young one had stole a petticoat from the old one, and was compelled to take it off and return it in the presence of at least fifty men. Left at 8, got to Tarboro at a quarter after nine.

April 26 — Left here this morning and took the same route that I came by. Our boat got to Greenville at 10 A.M. My regiment in my absence has gone twelve miles across the river to a place called Pacatolus. I followed them in a buggy, and got there at 4 P.M.

April 27 — Left here at 3 this morning. Got to Greenville at 6 A.M., stayed a quarter of an hour, and marched to the crossroads, nine miles from town; got there at 6 P.M.

April 28 — Turned about this morning at 7, got to Greenville at 10, and went to our former camp. Then got orders to return to Pacatolus in the morning.

April 29 — We left this morning. The regiment was two miles on the road when we got orders to return. But Tom Tiotter and myself marched ahead of the regiment, and had got four miles before we had found out that the regiment was not in our rear. When we got back we were laughed at for our smartness.

April 30 — Laid in camp and rested.

May 1 — We left here this morning at thirty minutes after 4 for Kinston. Marched eleven miles without halting.

May 2 — Resumed our march at 6 A.M., and reached Kinston at 8 P.M. — twenty-four miles to-day.

May 3 — We camped one mile from town. We left here on the 25th day of March, and returned May 2. Went through a campaign of twenty-seven days. In that time we had Washington besieged sixteen days. The balance of the time we were marching and counter-marching in all kinds of weather, and very often without anything to eat.

May 4 and 5 — Nothing.

May 6 — Left here at 12 M. for Core Creek, marched nine miles and halted. Raining hard, and we got well soaked. The rain ran down our faces all night, so we did not have to wash our faces on the morning of the 7th.

May 7 — Resumed our march at 8 A.M., got ten miles, and halted within one mile of the creek. We waded Gum Swamp, stayed there three hours, and turned about — marched nine miles to-night. This expedition was to tear up the Newbern and Kinston Railroad, and also bring some ladies and old men out of the Yankee lines, for they had been driven out of Newbern. There were about seventy in all. They were, of course, Southern people who would not take the oath of allegiance to the United States Government, and therefore were driven out of their homes.

May 8 — We left here at 8 A.M., to return to Kinston, and got there at 3 P.M. — ten miles — awful road. Waded through mud, water and sand the whole way. My feet are cut up pretty badly.

May 9 and 10 — Resting.

May 11 — We moved our camp to the north side of town. Then we were marched to an open field this afternoon, and drawn up in line to see two men shot for desertion. After they were shot, we marched by them and saw one was hit six times and the other four. Their coffins were by their sides, right close to their graves, so that they could see it all.

May 17 — Up to to-day nothing. But this morning at 4 we were ordered to cook up all our rations, and be ready to march in one hour. We left Kinston by rail at 12 M. Got to Goldsboro at 3, went through to Weldon, left here at 5 P.M., and got to Petersburg, Va., on the morning of the 18th; left there at 6 P.M. Katz and myself went uptown — ate two suppers. Had a very good time while in town. We camped all night on Dunn's Hill.

May 19 — Left here at 5 this morning, got to Richmond at 8, and are stationed at Camp Lee. We will have to march to Fredericksburg. Our brigade is transferred to the Army of Northern Virginia. William Cochran, myself and several of our company ran the blockade tonight, went uptown to a theatre, and got back to camp at 2 o'clock. We had a fine time while uptown.

May 21 — Left this morning, marched twenty-one miles, halted at 5.30. It is a very hilly country, warm and dusty.

May 22 — Marched twenty miles to-day, and halted at 6 P.M.

May 23 — Marched fifteen miles and halted. On our to-day's march we saw any amount of dead horses, which did not smell altogether like cologne.

May 24 — Laid here all day, it being Sunday.

May 25 — Resumed our march this morning at 6. Got six miles and halted. We pitched our camp here on a hill two miles from Fredericksburg.

May 26 and 27 — Rested. I went to see my brother Morris, who belongs to Dowles' Brigade, 44th Georgia Regiment. Did not see him, as he was on picket.

May 28 — Morris came to see me to-day. We are both in the same division and corps. Our corps is commanded by General Ewell.

May 29 — Had a general review to-day. General Rodes is our division commander. He and General Lee reviewed us. I see a great change in the appearance of General Lee. He looks so much older than when I saw him at Yorktown. Then his hair was black. Now he is a gray-headed old man. We have five brigades in our division. The commander of my brigade is General Daniels, of North Carolina. One brigade of Georgians is commanded by General Dowles. Iverson, of North Carolina, has another brigade; also General Ramseur, of North Carolina, has a brigade; and General Battle, of Alabama, has a brigade. Our corps is composed of three divisions, ours by General Rodes, one by General Early, and the other by Gen. A. Johnson.

June 30 — We see the Yankees in balloons every day, reconnoitering our lines.

June 1 and 2 — Nothing new.

June 3 — Saw my brother Morris several times.

June 4 — Got orders to cook three days' rations immediately. We left our camp at 3 this morning, marched fourteen miles and halted. We march one hour and rest ten minutes.

June 5 — Marched until 4 o'clock this evening — twenty miles to-day.

June 6 — Marched five miles and halted for the day.

June 7 — Left at 5 A.M., got to Culpepper Court House 3 P.M., and marched four miles on the east side of town. Twenty miles to-day. We waded Rapidan River, which is forty yards wide, two feet deep and very swift.

June 8 — Stayed here all day.

June 9 — We were ordered to Beverly Ford, to support Gen. Jeb Stewart, who is engaging the Yankees, and they are having a very hard cavalry fight. Got here in a roundabout way, and formed in line of battle, with two lines of skirmishers in front. When we got to the Army of Northern Virginia we were told that each company must furnish one skirmisher out of every six men, and there was a call for volunteers for that service. So I left the colors and went as a skirmisher, whose duty it is in time of battle to go in front of the line and reconnoitre and engage the enemy until a general engagement, then we fall in line with balance of the army. As soon as the enemy saw that the cavalry were reinforced by infantry, they fell back. This was altogether a cavalry fight. We took quite a number of prisoners, and camped two miles from the battlefield. We marched twelve miles to-day.

June 10 — Left here at 2 P.M., marched until 8 o'clock to-night — twelve miles.

June 11 — Resumed our march at 5 A.M., passed over three creeks that formed the Rappahannock River, passed through a town called Flint Hill, and camped one mile on the north side of the town. Marched sixteen miles to-day.

June 12 — Left at 5 A.M., marched over part of the Blue Ridge, and crossed the head of the Rappahannock River — eighteen miles to-day. We marched through Front Royal, where the ladies treated us very good. Camped one mile north side of town, and waded the Shaninoar, both prongs.

June 13 — Marched to Berryville, a Yankee post. Heard firing before we got there. We took the left flank a half mile this side of town, and marched to the Winchester Turnpike. We then formed in line of battle with sharp-shooters in front. We gave the rebel yell and charged. But when we got to their breastworks the birds had flown. They did not take their nests with them. Their camp, with all their cooking utensils, quartermaster and commissary stores, were all left in our hands. They were evidently cooking a meal, for plenty of pots full of eatables were still on the fire when we got into their camp. We ate up all we could, and filled our haversacks and pushed on four miles further, and halted for the night. It is raining very hard, and there is, of course, no shelter for us.

June 14 — Left at 7 A.M., passed through Smith-field and Bunker Hill. The Yankees are still retreating in our front, on their way to Martinsburg, our own destination. We got there about 9 o'clock at night and drove them through the town, and, in fact, we felt like driving the devil out of his stronghold, as this was a very warm day. We had to march in quick time all day, a distance of twenty-five miles. Therefore we were not in the best of humor. This is a good sized town.

June 15 — Left here at 11 A.M., and got to the Potomac river at dusk, a distance of twelve miles. We have as yet been very fortunate. Have driven the enemy from the Rapidan to the Potomac, captured prisoners, arms, camps, quartermaster and commissary stores, and the Yankees were any moment as strong in numbers as we, with the advantage of having breastworks to fight behind. Still they always ran at our appearance.

June 16 — Resting to-day.

June 17 — We crossed the Potomac River to-day at 1 P.M., and camped in Williamsport, Maryland, on the banks of the Potomac. Two miles to-day. The river is knee-deep.

June 18 — The people are mixed in their sympathies, some Confederates and some Yankees.

June 19 — Left at 8 A.M., and seven miles took us to Hagerstown, Md. Here the men greeted us very shabby, but the ladies quite the reverse. This town has 5,000 inhabitants, and is a very pretty town. We camped on the Antietam.

June 20 and 21 — Raining hard.

June 22 — Left this morning at 8 o'clock, got to Middleburg, Pa., at 11, passed through it, and got to Green Castle at half past one. Eleven miles to-day. The people seemed downhearted, and showed their hatred to us by their glum looks and silence, and I am willing to swear that no prayers will be offered in this town for us poor, ragged rebels.

June 23 — Here all day. Tom Tiotter and myself went out to buy something to eat, but when we came to a house, they would close their doors in our faces, or let us knock and not open. We got the ear of one or two ladies, and after proving to them that we were not wild animals nor thieves, they gave us what we wanted, but would not take pay for anything.

June 24 — Left here this morning, got to Chambersburg at 12 M. Went three miles on the north side of town on picket — 14 miles to-day. We passed through Marion, a small village. Chambersburg is a very fine place, 10,000 inhabitants, but nary a smile greeted us as we marched through town. There are a plenty of men here — a pity they are not rebels, and in our ranks. This city is in Franklin County, Cumberland Valley. We were woke up in the middle of the night and marched off; waded a river which was so cold that it woke us up. Passed through Greenville to-day at dawn. This town has, I should judge, about 5,000 inhabitants. Nine miles to-day.

June 25 — Marched on, passed through Leesburg, Canada, Hockinsville, and Centerville, all small villages. We got to Carlisle, Pa., at sundown. Marched 21 miles to-day. This city is certainly a beautiful place. It has 8,000 inhabitants, and we were treated very good by the ladies. They thought we would do as their soldiers do, burn every place we passed through, but when we told them the strict orders of General Lee they were rejoiced. Our regiment was provost guard in the city, but were relieved by the 21st Georgia Regiment, and we went to camp at the U.S.

barracks. So far we have lived very good in the enemy's country. We stayed here until the 30th, when we took the Baltimore pike road, crossed South Mountain at Holly Gap, passed through Papertown and Petersburg. We then left the Pike and took the Gettysburg road — 17 miles today. This has been a hard day for us, as we were the rear guard of the division, and it was very hot, close and very dusty, and a terrible job to keep the stragglers up.

July 1 — We left camp at 6 A.M., passed through Heidelsburg and Middleton. At the latter place we heard firing in the direction of Gettysburg. We were pushed forward after letting the wagon trains get in our rear. We got to Gettysburg at 1 P.M., 15 miles. We were drawn up in line of battle about one mile south of town, and a little to the left of the Lutheran Seminary. We then advanced to the enemy's line of battle in double quick time. We had not gotten more than 50 paces when Norman of our company fell dead by my side. Katz was going to pick him up. I stopped him, as it is strictly forbidden for any one to help take the dead or wounded off the field except the ambulance corps. We then crossed over a rail fence, where our Lieutenant McMatthews and Lieutenant Alexander were both wounded. That left us with a captain and one lieutenant. After this we got into battle in earnest, and lost in our company very heavily, both killed and wounded. This fight lasted four hours and a half, when at last we drove them clear out of town, and took at least 3,000 prisoners. They also lost very heavily in killed and wounded, which all fell into our hands. After the fight our company was ordered to pick up all straggling Yankees in town, and bring them together to be brought to the rear as prisoners. One fellow I took up could not speak one word of English, and the first thing he asked me in German was, "Will I get my pay in prison?" After we had them all put up in a pen we went to our regiment and rested. Major Iredell, of our regiment, came to me and shook my hand, and also complimented me for action in the fight. At dusk I was about going to hunt up my brother Morris, when he came to me. Thank God, we are both safe as yet. We laid all night among the dead Yankees, but they did not disturb our peaceful slumbers.

July 2 — Our division was in reserve until dark, but our regiment was supporting a battery all day. We lost several killed and wounded, although we had no chance to fire — only lay by a battery of artillery and be shot at. The caisson of the battery we were supporting was blown up and we got a big good sprinkling of the wood from it. Just at dark we were sent to the front under terrible cannonading. Still, it was certainly a beautiful sight. It being dark, we could see the cannon vomit forth fire. Our company had to cross a rail fence. It gave way and several of our boys were hurt by others walking over them. We laid down here a short time, in fact no longer than 10 minutes, when I positively fell asleep. The cannonading did not disturb me. One of the boys shook me and told me Katz was wounded by a piece of a shell striking him on the side, and he was sent to the rear. We went on to the Baltimore Turnpike until 3 in the morning of the 3d.

July 3 — When under a very heavy fire, we were ordered on Culps Hill, to the support of Gen. A. Johnson. Here we stayed all day — no, here, I may say, we melted away. We were on the brow of one hill, the enemy on the brow of another. We charged on them several times, but of course, running down our hill, and then to get to them was impossible, and every time we attempted it we came back leaving some of our comrades behind. Here our Lieutenant Belt lost his arm. We have now in our company a captain. All of our lieutenants are wounded. We fought here until 7 P.M., when what was left of us was withdrawn and taken to the first day's battlefield. At the commencement of this fight our brigade was the strongest in our division, but she is not now. We lost the most men, for we were in the fight all the time, and I have it from Colonel Owens that our regiment lost the most in the brigade. I know that our company went in the fight with 60 men. When we left Culps Hill there were 16 of us that answered to the roll call. The balance were all killed and wounded. There were 12 sharpshooters in our company and now John Cochran and myself are the only ones that are left. This day none will forget, that participated in the fight. It was truly awful how fast, how very fast, did our poor boys fall by our sides — almost as fast as the leaves that fell as cannon and musket balls hit them, as they flew on their deadly errand. You could see one with his head shot off, others cut in two, then one with his brain oozing out, one with his leg off, others shot through the heart. Then you would hear some poor friend or foe crying for water, or for "God's sake" to kill him. You would see some of your comrades, shot through the leg, lying between the lines, asking his friends to take him out, but no one could get to his relief, and you would have to leave him there, perhaps to die, or, at best, to become a prisoner. Our brigade was the only one that was sent to Culps Hill to support General Johnson. In our rapid firing today my gun became so hot that the ramrod would not come out, so I shot it at the Yankees, and picked up a gun from the ground, a gun that some poor comrade dropped after being shot. I wonder if it hit a Yankee; if so, I pity him. Our regiment was in a very exposed position at one time to-day, and our General

Daniels ordered a courier of his to bring us from the hill. He was killed before he got to us. The General sent another. He was also killed before he reached us. Then General Daniels would not order any one, but called for volunteers. Capt. Ed. Stitt, of Charlotte, one of his aides, responded, and he took us out of the exposed position.

July 4 — We laid on the battlefield of the first day, this the fourth day of July. No fighting to-day, but we are burying the dead. They have been lying on the field in the sun since the first day's fight; it being dusty and hot, the dead smell terribly. The funny part of it is, the Yankees have all turned black. Several of our company, wounded, have died. Katz is getting along all right. The battle is over, and although we did not succeed in pushing the enemy out of their strong position, I am sure they have not anything to boast about. They have lost at least as many in killed and wounded as we have. We have taken more prisoners from them than they have from us. If that is not the case, why did they lay still all today and see our army going to the rear? An army that has gained a great victory follows it up while its enemy is badly crippled; but Meade, their commander, knows he has had as much as he gave, at least, if not more. As yet I have not heard a word from my brother Morris since the first day's fight.

July 5 — Left this morning at 5 o'clock. Only marched ten miles to-day. The enemy being in our rear, and skirmishing very strong.

July 6 — Our company was ordered out as skirmishers to-day, as our regular skirmish corps was broken up during the fight. We were the rear of the army, and therefore had a very hard job before us. Fighting all day in falling back we certainly had fun. We were close enough to the enemy to hear their commands. We would hold them in check and give them a few rounds, then fall back again. They would then advance until we would make a stand, fight again, and so it was until we reached Fairfield, six miles from Gettysburg. I don't think there were many lost on either side in this skirmish. We crossed South Mountain at Monteray Gap. When we came to the above town I pressed into service a citizen's coat, in this way: We were ordered to rest, and, as usual, we would sit on fences and lay about the road. Some of the boys jumped on an old hog pen. It broke through. They fell in, and, lo and behold, there were boxes of clothing, dresses, shawls, blankets, and, in fact, everything in the line of wearing apparel. I, being a little fellow, crawled through some of the boys' legs and captured the coat. If the fool citizen would have left his things in his house they would have been safe, but to put it in our way was too much for us to leave behind. We also passed through Waterboro, and Waynesboro, Pa., where the Maryland line commences. We then passed through Latisburg, and halted in Hagerstown, Md., on the evening of the 7th. We marched yesterday and all night up to 11 o'clock — twenty-four miles.

July 8 — We are resting, and, goodness knows, we need it very much. I sold my coat for twenty dollars and a gray jacket. We lost in the last fight in our company eleven killed and twenty-six wounded; three of the latter will not live, and nine of our number became prisoners, besides the wounded. Our three lieutenants are all wounded and prisoners. Katz is also a prisoner. Nothing further up to the 10th.

July 10 — Moved four and a half miles on the other side of town. We have fortified ourselves here.

July 11 — Orders read out to-day from our father,

R. E. Lee, that we would fight the enemy once more on their own soil, as they were now in our front. That order got to them, and fulfilled its mission, as we were then on our way to the Potomac. They still thinking we could not cross the river, because the river was very high from the recent rains, and we had but one pontoon bridge. At 10 in the night we formed in line of battle, got to our position, when our regiment was ordered to support a battery. Laid on our arms all night.

July 12 — Went back to our brigade this morning. Skirmishing very heavy on the left and center.

July 13 — News came to us to-day that Vicksburg had fallen on the 4th. Heavy skirmishing, fighting all day. Our brigade again acted as the rear of our corps, our regiment being its rear. We started our retreat at dark and marched to Williamsport, six miles, through mud and slush ankle-deep, and raining very hard. We marched one mile to the right of and crossed the Potomac at midnight, after wading through the canal, which we destroyed. The river was up to my chin, and very swift. We crossed in fours, for protection, as otherwise we could not have crossed. Our cartridge boxes we carried around our necks to keep the powder dry. On the south bank tar was poured so that we would not slip back in the river, as the mud was very slick. J. Engle, of our company, was stuck in until some of the boys pulled him out. We went six miles further, and I honestly believe more of us were asleep on our night's march than awake. But, still, all kept up, for the rear was prison. We then halted, made fire to dry ourselves, just as day was breaking on the morning of the 14th.

July 14 — The roads are so bad that it is hard work to trudge along. I stuck in the mud several times, and lost one shoe in a mud hole, but of course took it out again. One consolation we have got, it is raining so hard that the mud is washed off our clothing, therefore they were not soiled too bad. But the devil of it is there is no blacking to shine our shoes with. Marched sixteen miles and halted. We are now, thank God, on Confederate soil, but oh, how many of our dear comrades have we left behind. We can never forget this campaign. We had hard marching, hard fighting, suffered hunger and privation, but our general officers were always with us, to help the weary soldier carry his gun, or let him ride. In a fight they were with us to encourage. Many a general have I seen walk and a poor sick private riding his horse, and our father, Lee, was scarcely ever out of sight when there was danger. We could not feel gloomy when we saw his old gray head uncovered as he would pass us on the march, or be with us in a fight. I care not how weary or hungry we were, when we saw him we gave that rebel yell, and hunger and wounds would be forgotten.

July 15 — We marched five miles to-day, and were compelled to halt, as our wagon trains had to get in our front. I and two of our mess killed three turkeys, took them with us to one mile from Martinsburg, Va., where we camped, and the bones of those turkeys were left behind.

July 16 — Left this morning at 7; marched to Darkesville, eight miles.

July 17 — Raining very hard to-day, and we are resting.

July 20 — Went on picket to-day, stayed there one hour, and was ordered back. Got to camp, and found our brigade gone. We marched to Martinsburg, halted at 10 at night, two miles from town — ten miles to-day.

July 21 — Went through town at 5 this morning,

to the Baltimore and Ohio Railroad, with Johnson's division and part of Hampton's Legion, to tear up the railroad. We destroyed six miles of it and returned to our camp at Darkesville — fifteen miles to-day.

July 22 — Left this morning at 5, marched through Winchester three miles, and halted.

July 23 — Left at 5 this morning, went through Front Royal — seventeen miles to-day. Waded the south and north prongs of the Shenandoah River. We then took the road to Mananas Gap, marched three miles, when we met the enemy and had brisk firing until dark. Their line is very strong. They advanced in two lines in very fine order. When they got within range of our guns we opened on them, and they scattered like bluebirds. We had a beautiful view of this fight, as we are on the mountain. Neither of the armies can move without being seen by the other. Our corps of sharpshooters has been formed again since a few days ago. We were sent to the support of the other corps. We were within twenty yards of the enemy's line until midnight, when we fell back in good order.

July 24 — Marched two miles up Chester Gap, when we were about faced and marched through Front Royal again. We here took the Strasburg road at daylight. We resumed our march, and halted at 3 in the evening. We have been on a forced march three days and nights, waded rivers, fought skirmishes, and marched in that time forty-five miles. We are camped in an apple orchard in a village called Milford.

July 25 — Left this morning at 7 o'clock, halted at 3 in the afternoon — sixteen miles.

July 26 — Rested to-day. William Eagle and myself went up the Blue Ridge to gather berries, and were lost in the woods for one hour.

July 27 — Left this morning at 5, crossed the Blue Ridge at Thornton Gap. We camped one mile from Sparrowsville. Marched thirteen miles to-day.

July 28 — Left at 6 this morning, marched ten miles and halted on the mountain.

July 29 — Left at 7, marched until 3, camped one mile from Madison Court House. Marched ten miles to-day.

July 30 — Still in camp. Hugh Sample and myself were out on a forage and milked a cow in his hat, the only thing we had.

July 31 — We left here to-night, marched seven miles, and halted.

August 1 — Resumed our march at 4 this morning, and got to Orange Court House, fourteen miles. It is a very hot day, and there were several men fell dead on the road from sunstroke. We rested here until the 4th.

August 4 — Left our camp, marched three miles, one mile on the south side of town.

August 11 — Nothing up to to-day. This, I suppose, is to be our regular camp, as we have commenced to drill again.

August 12 — We had a very severe storm to-day, which killed two men and hurt several of our brigade. It tore up trees and played smash in general.

August 23 — They have commenced to give furloughs, one to every two companies.

August 24 — Was on guard this morning, but Sergeant Hugh Reid sent for me, and detailed me, with some men out of every regiment in our brigade, to hunt deserters. Si Wolf and myself, out of our company. We left camp at 3 this evening, marched two miles up the railroad, and took the cars to Gordonsville. Got there at 4. It is a small place, but one of importance, as all our supplies for the army from Richmond come from this station.

August 25 — Took the cars at 5 A.M. and got to Keswick, a depot on the Stanton road. We left here after staying one hour, and took our posts in the woods. As we are about twenty men, with one lieutenant in command, we made no camp, but stayed about here and reported every time there was any news about deserters. Wolf and myself went out in the country to houses that we were told harbored deserters. We passed ourselves off as such, and were well received, and got some valuable information. They told us that the deserters were in the woods. We then returned to our companions, and got well soaked, as it was raining very hard. Stayed in a barn all night.

August 26 — We stayed in the woods all day, but at night went out scouting for deserters, but did not find any.

August 27 — Returned at 7 this morning, went out again at dark, went through four houses of bad repute, but found not one deserter. Went twelve miles this night.

August 28 — We moved this evening, and I stayed in a gentleman's house all night with Wolf.

August 29 — Returned to our companions this morning at 10 o'clock.

August 30 — Left at 5 in the morning. We hunted through the cliffs for several hours and caught one deserter. Several of our men and myself dined in a widow lady's house. There were quite a number of ladies there, and we had a very pleasant time. Then we went to Mr. Bell's and had supper there. From there we went to Mr. Wheeler's and stayed all night.

August 31 — Went to Mr. Watkin's, took dinner there, and stayed all day. Had a very pleasant time with his daughter, Miss Annie.

September 1 — To-day we went on a general hunt in full force. We went into a house where we suspected there was a deserter. We hunted through all the out-houses, then went to the house, and the lady strongly denied there being any one there, but would not give us permission to look. We then searched the house, but found no one. I then proposed that we go in the loft. She objected again. But of course we were determined. It was pitch-dark in the loft. We called in, but no answer came. I then proposed, in a loud voice, so that if any one was there they could hear me, that we fix bayonets and stick around and satisfy ourselves that no one was there. Still no answer. I then got in the loft, took my gun and commenced sticking around. At last an answer came from the far corner that he would surrender. The way I got into the loft was, I being a little fellow, and Si Wolf a tall man, they put me on his shoulder, and in that way I crawled in. We then left for camp, passed a church, and was in time to see a wedding. We drilled for the ladies, and had a good time.

September 2 — On a hunt to-day several of my comrades with myself came to a house, and the first thing we heard was, "Is there a Jew in your detachment that caught a deserter yesterday?" They would like to see him, etc. At last one of the boys told them that I was the Jew. After that I had a very good time there, and in fact wherever I went I was received very kindly, and was very sorry to see on the 4th that orders came for us to return to our brigade.

September 4 — Marched to Keswick, and found that we would have to march to Gordonsville. Got there that night. Fifteen miles to-day.

September 5 — Left here at 7, got to brigade at 10

in the morning, and from the 24th of last month up to date I certainly have seen the best time since the war.

September 6 — Our captain, Harvey White, returned to camp yesterday from a furlough.

September 8 — We are getting ready for a corps review for to-morrow.

September 9 — To-day we had a review. Present: General Lee, General Ewell, General Early, General Johnson and General Rodes, of our corps, and General Hill, Gen. J.E.B. Stewart, and smaller fry of our army. It was certainly a grand scene. Nothing more up to the 14th.

September 14 — Left camp this morning at 7, marched twelve miles and halted. Hear firing in front on the Rapidan, at Summerville Ford. Here all night.

September 15 — Still some firing in front. We are in reserve. I went to see the fight. I saw the enemy very plainly, and thus I spent my New Year's Day.

September 16 — To-day there was a man shot for desertion. Eight balls passed through him. The way this is conducted is: the brigade that he belongs to, or sometimes even the division, is drawn up in full sight of the doomed man. He is tied to a stake in front of his grave, which is already dug, and his coffin at his side. There is a squad of twelve men and one officer detailed to do the shooting. Eleven of the guns are loaded. The guns are given to them by the officer, so that no man knows which gun is loaded. The order is then given to fire. Thus ends the deserter's life. The brigade, or division, then marches around him, so that every man can see his, the deserter's, end.

September 17 — Very little firing to-day.

September 18 — Raining hard all day, and no tents. Left camp at 2 in the afternoon, marched six miles, halted at the river, and our regiment went on picket. It is still raining very hard, and we are as wet as drowned cats, and cold, too, for we cannot make a fire in front of the enemy. If we did they would have a good mark to shoot at.

September 19 — We are at Moulton's Ford.

September 20 — In speaking distance of the Yankees.

September 21 — Our regiment was relieved to-day by the 3d Alabama, of Battle's Brigade.

September 22 — I spoke and exchanged papers with a Yankee of the 7th Ohio Regiment.

September 23 — Day of Atonement to-day. Nothing more up to the 26th.

September 26 — We have built ourselves cabins in our camps. This evening we went on picket.

September 27 — The Yankees are very active to-day. Something is up.

September 28 — Our regiment is on picket; will be relieved to-morrow.

September 29 — All quiet to-day. Brother Morris returned from Richmond yesterday, where he has been for ten days on a furlough. Before our Jewish New Year there was an order read out from General Lee granting a furlough to each Israelite to go to Richmond for the holidays if he so desired. I did not care to go.

September 30 — We are shooting at the Yankees to-day for fun, as they are trying to steal sheep from the houses that are between our lines.

October 1 — Went on picket at 4 this afternoon, and was roused up in the night to intercept a spy who is in our lines, and is expecting to cross, but we did not see him, for it was so dark we could see nothing.

October 2 — Relieved to-day. Very wet and disagreeable weather. Nothing new up to the 9th.

October 9 — Left camp at 4 this evening and halted on the morning of the 10th at 1 o'clock, when we caught up with our brigade. Marched twelve miles on very muddy road, and fell into several holes. We left again very early this morning and marched twenty miles. We waded the Rapidan to-day at Liberty Mills.

October 11 — We forded Roberson River, and marched up and down hollows without singing or making any noise, so that the enemy could not see or hear us. We heard firing on our left. We are eight miles from Culpepper Court House.

October 12 — Started at daylight, marched twenty-five miles, waded the Hazel River at 10 this morning. Had to take off our shoes and pants, according to orders. It was very cold. We got within a quarter of a mile of Jefferson town, when the fight commenced. We drove the Yankees through town double quick. We halted one mile on the other side of the town, then formed in line of battle once more and went forward. We drove the enemy over the Rappahannock and through Warrington Springs; took 300 prisoners and halted at 9 in the night.

October 13 — Left here at daylight, marched through Warrington, a very handsome place, went two miles further and camped for the night — seven miles.

October 14 — My corps of sharpshooters marched in front of the line. Left camp at 4 this morning, and at daylight, as General Ewell and staff rode up to us, there was a volley shot at us. We immediately deployed and after the enemy. We fought on a run for six hours, all the time the enemy falling back. They at one time raised a white flag and surrendered. We then stopped firing, and as we got within one hundred feet they opened on us again, for they saw we were only a line of sharpshooters. We then resumed firing at them. I captured a mail-bag in the fight, and in several letters I found some money. We halted, and the enemy kept on running like wild ducks. This is the battle of Bristow Station. We took many prisoners. As we got through fighting we heard firing on our right. We marched to their support, but when we got there the firing had ceased. Twenty-five miles to-day. We camped on Manassas Plain. Raining hard all night.

October 15 — Here all day, and talking with our prisoners.

October 16 — Left this morning at 4, marched five miles, and halted on the Orange and Alexander Railroad, tore it up one and a quarter miles, and camped.

October 17 — Marched four miles to-day and tore and burned up the same amount of railroad.

October 18 — Started at 4 this morning and marched ten miles toward Culpepper Court House. We tore up the railroad from Manassas to the Rappahannock River. The way we tear up railroads is this: we take the cross-ties and make a square of them as high as your head. We place the rails on the cross-ties, then set it afire and the rails bend double.

October 19 — Left at 4 this morning, crossed the river on pontoon bridges. It commenced to hail and rain very hard, and kept it up for two hours. We got very wet. Halted at Cedar Run, marched ten miles, and stayed here until the 21st.

October 21 — We were sent to Kelly's Ford on picket.

October 22 — Relieved to-day. It was bitter cold.

October 23 — We commenced putting up winter quarters, and were hard at work up till the last of this month.

November 1 — Moved into our shanties to-day. There are five of us in mine. They are ten feet square.

November 3 — Went on picket on the Rappahannock at Norman's Ford, six miles from camp.

November 6 — Were relieved to-day.

November 7 — To-day, as several of us went to get some straw near Kelly's Ford, we heard firing, and the long roll beat. Looking up we saw the Yankees crossing the river. We double-quicked to camp and got there just in time to fall in with our regiment, to intercept the enemy, but they had already crossed the river before we got there. We maneuvered about until dark, when my corps of sharp-shooters was ordered out. We were within one hundred yards of the Yankees, and saw them around their fires very plainly. On the morning of the 8th we retreated in very good order. I certainly was glad of it, as we were in a very bad fix. We marched until sun-up and halted on Stone Mountain, passed through Stevensburg. Stayed here all night, and resumed our march and halted on the morning of the 9th. We then crossed the Rapidan at the Raccoon Ford, and are now camped at our old camp at Moulton Ford. We marched, since leaving Kelly's Ford, forty miles. The distance is only seventeen miles. We were certainly surprised for the first time since the war. We did not dream the enemy was on us before the firing commenced. Our brigade was cut off from the army twice, but our General Daniels got us through safe. Nothing new up to the 26th.

November 26 — When we had marched seven miles we heard cannonading. The enemy is trying to cross the river at Jacob's Ford, but our boys kept them back. We laid in breastworks of our own make until the 27th.

November 27 — This morning we marched seven miles, halted a short time, and resumed our march. Got three miles further, and firing commenced in our front. We then counter-marched and formed in line of battle, in the edge of the woods. One corps of sharpshooters was sent out to find the enemy. Fought the enemy one-half hour and were forced back. My corps then went out as reinforcement. We fought then for four hours, and were called back to our command. I, at one time in this fight, was in a close place. Being in front, I did not hear the order to fall back, and being by myself was left a target for a dozen Yankees, but my Captain White saw what a fix I was in and sent a squad of our company to my relief, so I fell back with them. We then, that night, went to Mine Run and formed our line of battle there.

November 28 — To-day the whole army is throwing up breastworks. The sharpshooters are out in front, my corps out to-day. We made ourselves small pits to lay in as a protection from the Yankee bullets. These pits are just about large enough to hold two or three men. Pinkney King, Sam Wilson and myself are in one. We are shooting at the enemy all day. They are returning the compliment. Late this evening we saw some of them opposite our pits, trying to get into a house. We jumped out of our pits and fired at them several times, when poor King was shot and died in a few minutes. Another man was sent to relieve in his place, and we held our position. The other corps of sharpshooters fought all day.

November 29 — Ours again to-day, but not as hard as before, but heavy enough. The cannonading is getting heavier.

December 1 — The other corps is out to-day. The Yankees, as well as ourselves, are well fortified, and we are confronting one another.

December 2 — This morning at 3 we moved to the right until daylight, when our corps was again sent to the front. We advanced toward the enemy's works. We moved, of course, very carefully, as we saw their breastworks, and in front of us two cannon. When we got in shooting range, the order was given to "Charge!" We did so with a rebel yell, and as we got upon their breastworks, lo and behold, there were no Yankees, and the cannons we saw were nothing but logs. We followed them to the river, but their whole army had crossed. We, of course, captured a great many of their sick and stragglers.

December 3 — Marched back to our camp at Moulton's Ford, and our regiment was sent on picket at Mitchell's Ford, seven miles from camp. This has been a very severe seven-days' campaign, as we fought mostly all the time. Cold, sleety, disagreeable weather, and we dare not make large fires, as that would be a sure target for the Yankees. Mine Run is a small stream on the Orange and Fredericksburg turnpike. Nothing more worth recording up to the 8th, my birthday, and spent it as dull as could be. Have been on picket, and relieved on Dole's Georgia Brigade. Up to the 27th nothing doing.

December 27 — We moved our camps from our picket posts seven miles from Orange Court House. On the turnpike from there to Fredericksburg, and commenced putting up winter quarters. On the 31st moved into them, and for the first time in a year or two we have with our rations some coffee, sugar and dried apples.

CHAPTER THREE
The Year 1864

January 8 — It has been snowing, and is very cold. Some of the boys have formed a dramatic company, and I went to see them play "Toodles." There were two men shot in our brigade for desertion to-day. Nothing of interest until 11th.

January 11 — Left our camp at sun-up, got five miles and halted in the woods. We have been detailed to run two sawmills, and we are now putting up winter quarters there.

January 16 — Nothing more until to-day. W. R. Berryhill has got the smallpox. Quite a number of us were in the same quarters with him, but none of us caught the disease. I was detailed to work at the mills, and therefore I am learning a new trade. Live and learn.

January 20 — Hard work until to-day, when we were sent out to lay a plank road. While at work General Lee and his daughter rode by us, and soon after a courier came from his headquarters and gave us some woolen socks and gloves — sent to us from his daughter. Nothing more worth recording this month.

February 2 — While hard at work in the woods, hauling stocks for the mill, my furlough came, for eighteen days. So I was relieved. On the 3d I left camp and got home on the morning of the 6th. It took me several days to get accustomed to living as a civilian, as I have been in camp for two years at a stretch. I had a very good time, and will always be grateful for the kindness shown me by every one while at home.

February 23 — Reached camp to-day, and found that my regiment had marched once since I left. This was the first I missed since my regiment was formed. Nothing more this month.

March 1 — Raining hard. Left camp at 9 this morning, halted at dark nine miles from Madison Court House. Snowing to-night. We had a hard road to travel, and when we got to our destination the enemy had gone.

March 2 — Started back to camp. The weather was clear and cold. Got there at 7 in the evening, and I stiff from walking. We marched eighteen miles to-day.

March 3 — Left camp at 8 this morning to intercept General Kilpatrick, who is scouting in our lines. We formed in line of battle, had all the roads guarded, when we found out that he was already on his way to the peninsula, so we returned to camp. Twenty miles to-day.

March 4 — I am as stiff as an old man this morning from yesterday's march on the plank road.

March 5 — We left the mills this morning and returned to our brigade, a distance of five miles. Nothing more up to the 17th.

March 17 — An order was read out at dress parade that all troops in the army would be held until the end of the war. This was nothing of importance to us, as we enlisted for that time. It is raining and snowing very hard, and almost every day. Our regiment is not in winter quarters, for we expect to move when the bad weather stops. We had a snowball fight — our regiment with the 43d North Carolina. Then our brigade with Battle's Brigade. It was lots of fun. Nothing more until the 26th.

March 26 — We were visited to-day by our Governor, Zeb Vance, who made us a speech of two and a half hour's duration. With him on the platform was General Lee, General Ewell and several others.

March 28 — We were reviewed to-day by our Governor. When I say reviewed, I mean all the North Carolina troops in our corps. After the review we went to Ramseur's Brigade, where he spoke again. So did Generals Early, Rodes and Stewart. That is all that is worth recording this month.

April 1 — Left camp at 8 this morning to go on picket twelve miles from our camp. Our brigade went on picket at Raccoon Ford, and picketed up to Moulton's Ford. Raining hard to-day, also on the 2d. The river is ten feet above common watermark.

April 3 — As I have not heard from my parents since the war, they living in New York, I thought I would send a personal advertisement to a New York paper to let them know that my brother and myself are well, and for them to send an answer through the Richmond paper. I gave this to a Yankee picket, who promised me he would send it to New York. Nothing more up to the 7th.

April 7 — This is a day of fasting and prayer, set apart by President Davis.

April 9 — Were relieved to-day by Doles' Georgia Brigade. Got to camp at 1 in the evening, raining very hard all day. Nothing more up to the 14th.

April 14 — I went to A.P. Hill's corps to visit my friend, Lieutenant Rusler, and returned to camp on the 15th.

April 15 — Nothing more up to the 18th.

April 18 — Our corps of sharpshooters went out today target practising. We shoot a distance of 500 yards offhand. Some very good shooting was done.

April 20 — I hit the bull's-eye to-day. We are practising every day up to the 23d.

April 23 — Went to Moulton's Ford, met Stonewall Brigade on our way, and had some lively talk with them, all in fun, of course. Stayed on picket until 30th, then we were relieved at 11 in the morning, and reached camp at 2.

May 1 — Rumors are flying that we will soon get hard fighting. Nothing more up to the 4th.

May 4 — This morning we got orders to be ready at a moment's notice. Broke camp at noon, marched to our old breastworks at Mine Run, seven miles from camp. Rested two hours, and moved forward toward the river three miles further and halted.

May 5 — Moved this morning, feeling for the enemy, and came up to them at noon, five miles from the Run, in the Wilderness. It certainly is a wilderness; it is almost impossible for a man to walk, as the woods are thick with an underbrush growth and all kinds of shrubbery, old logs, grapevines, and goodness knows what. My corps of sharpshooters was ordered to the front. We formed in line and advanced to the enemy. We fought them very hard for three hours, they falling back all the time. Our sharpshooters' line got mixed up with Gordon's Brigade, and fought with them. In one charge we got to the most elevated place in the Wilderness. We looked back for our brigade, but saw it not. Just then a Yankee officer came up and we took him prisoner. Some of Gordon's men took him to the rear. Six of our regiment, sharp-shooters, myself included, went to the right to join our regiment, but were picked up by the Yankees and made prisoners. We were run back in their line on the double quick. When we got to their rear we found about 300 of our men were already prisoners. The Yankees lost very heavily in this fight, more than we did. Although we lost heavy enough, but, my Heavens! what an army they have got. It seems to me that there is ten of them to one of us. It looks strange that we could deliver such fearful blows when, in fact, if numbers counted, they should have killed us two years ago. In going to their rear we passed through four lines of battle and reinforcements still coming up, while we are satisfied with, or at least have no more than one line of battle.

May 6 — Fighting commenced at daylight, and lasted all day. So did it last with their everlasting reinforcements. If General Lee only had half their men, and those men were rebels, we would go to Washington in two weeks. When he has fought such an army for four years it certainly shows we have the generals and the fighting-stock on our side, and they have the hirelings. Look at our army, and you will see them in rags and bare-footed. But among the Yankees I see nothing but an abundance of everything. Still, they haven't whipped the rebels. Several of our boys came in as prisoners to-day, with them Engle of our company. They think I was killed, so does my brother, but as yet the bullet has not done its last work for your humble servant.

May 7 — We are still penned up as prisoners in the rear of the army, close by General Grant's headquarters.

A great many prisoners came in to-day. From some of them I heard that my brother was well.

May 8 — We left this place at dark last night, but only got a distance of two miles, and it took us until 9 in the morning of the 9th.

May 9 — Started again this morning, and passed over the Chancellorsville battlefield. Marched twelve miles to-day. We passed a brigade of negro troops. They gave us a terrible cursing, and hollered "Fort Pillow" at us. I am only sorry that this brigade of negroes was not there, then they certainly would not curse us now. We halted at dark on the plank road seven miles from Fredericksburg.

May 10 — Fighting to-day at Spottsylvania Court House. Prisoners still coming in, two more from my company.

May 11 — This morning about 800 more prisoners came in. Most of them were from my brigade, as well as from Dole's Georgians. I was surprised to see my brother with them. He was taken yesterday, but before he surrendered he sent two of the enemy to their long home with his bayonet.

May 12 — Raining hard all day, and fighting all last night. About 2 o'clock this afternoon about 2,000 prisoners came in, with them Major-General Johnson and Brigadier-General Stewart. We have moved four miles nearer to Fredericksburg. I suppose they think we are too close to our own lines, and they are afraid we will be re-captured, as it was a few days ago. We heard our boys', or, as the Yankees call it, the rebel yell. We prisoners also gave the rebel yell. A few minutes after that they brought cannon to bear on us, and we were told to stop, or they would open on us. We stopped.

May 13 — Left here this morning and passed

through Fredericksburg. Crossed the Rappahannock on pontoon bridges, and got to Belle Plain on the Potomac at 3 o'clock — nineteen miles to-day. It rained all day, and it is very muddy.

May 14 — We are still camped here. Have been prisoners since the 5th of this month, and have drawn three and a half days' rations. On that kind of a diet I am not getting very fat. We certainly would have suffered a great deal, but our Yankee guard gave us quite a lot of their own rations.

May 15 — Still here. They are fighting very hard on the front.

May 16 — Left this morning at 11 in a tugboat, and from here packed into the Steamer *S. R. Spaulding.* We are now on our way to a regular prison. We got there at 8 o'clock to-night, and found it to be Point Lookout, Md., fifty miles from Belle Plain. It is in St. Mary's County. We were drawn up in line, searched for valuables, and they taken from us, and marched to prison, one mile from the landing. There are sixteen men in each tent.

May 17 — Saw Mack Sample, Will Stone and several of our company to-day that have been prisoners since the battle of Gettysburg. We get two meals a day.

May 18 — We are divided in divisions and companies. There is a thousand in each division and one hundred in each company. A sergeant commands each company. We get light bread one day and crackers the other.

May 19 — Saw Darnell, of my company, to-day. He was just from the front. He brings us very bad news. Our General Daniels was killed, which is certainly a great loss to us, for he was a good and brave man, also our major of the 53d, Iredell, and my captain, White, all killed. Colonel Owens, my colonel, was mortally wounded, and quite a number of my company were killed and wounded. He says there is only seven of our company left, and that our Lieutenant-Colonel Morehead is commanding Daniels' Brigade.

May 20 — Three years ago to-day the Old North State left the Union, and we went to the front full of hopes to speedily show the Yankee Government that the South had a right to leave the Union; but to-day, how dark it looks!

May 21 — I heard to-day that my brother Morris was a prisoner at Fort Delaware, Pa. I asked for a parole to-day to go and see my parents in New York, but they could not see it.

May 22 — Nothing new from the front.

May 23 — We are guarded by negro troops, who are as mean as hell. At each meal there is a guard placed over 500 prisoners, who go to their meals in ranks of four. We are not allowed to cross a certain line, called the "Dead Line," but as 500 men go at one time to meals, of course near the door there is always a rush. To-day one of our men accidentally crossed the line. He was pushed over by the crowd, when a black devil shot and killed him, and wounded two others.

May 24 — One of yesterday's wounded died to-day. This negro company was taken away to-day, as there is no telling what even men without arms will do to such devils, although they have got guns.

May 25 — Engle received a letter from his father today, who told him they had seen my parents, and I would hear from them soon. This is the first time that I have heard about my parents since the commencement of the war. Thank God, my parents, as well as my sisters and brothers, are well.

May 26 — Received two letters to-day, one from home and one from my brother Pincus, who went to Washington on his way to visit Morris and myself, as he has to get a pass from headquarters before he can see us. He was refused and returned home. Our daily labor as prisoners is that at 5 in the morning we have roll call; 6, breakfast, 500 at a time, as one lot gets through another takes its place, until four lots have eaten; we then stroll about the prison until 1 o'clock, when we eat dinner in the same style as breakfast, then loaf about again until sundown. Roll is called again, thus ending the day. We get for breakfast five crackers with worms in them; as a substitute for butter, a small piece of pork, and a tin cup full of coffee; dinner, four of the above crackers, a quarter of a pound mule meat and a cup of bean soup, and every fourth day an eight-ounce loaf of white bread. Nothing more this month.

June 8 — There is nothing new up to to-day, when I received a box of eatables, one or two shirts, and one pair of pants from home. The only way we can pass our time off is playing cards and chess. Six hundred prisoners came in to-day, with them a lady, who is an artillery sergeant. Being questioned by the provost marshal, she said she could straddle a horse, jump a fence and kill a Yankee as well as any rebel. As time in prison is very dull and always the same thing as the day preceding, I shall not mention each day, but only those days upon which something happened.

June 11 — Five hundred more prisoners came in to-day.

June 12 — To-day, as the negro guard was relieved, two of them commenced playing with their guns and bayonets, sticking at one another. Fortunately one of their guns, by accident, went off and made a hole in the other one's body, which killed him instantly. The other one kicked at him several times, telling him to get up as the rebels were laughing at him, but in a very short time he found out that he had killed his comrade and that we were laughing sure enough.

June 27 — Received money to-day from home, but they gave me sutler's checks for it, as we were not allowed any money, for fear we would bribe the sentinels and make our escape.

July 4 — Four hundred prisoners left here for some other prison, as there were too many here.

July 8 — Engle, Riter and myself received boxes from New York to-day, but as Riter has gone to the other prison with the 400 we have made away with his box.

July 23 — Three hundred more were sent from here to the new prison, which is in Elmira, N.Y., myself with them.

July 25 — Left Point Lookout at 8 o'clock this evening in the frigate *Victor* for New York. There are 700 prisoners on board.

July 26 — To-day on the ocean a great many of our boys were seasick, but not I. I was promised a guard to take me to see my parents in New York for thirty minutes.

July 27 — We see the Jersey shore this morning. Our vessel was racing with another. We had too much steam up; the consequence was a fire on board, but we soon had it out. We landed at Jersey City at 12 M., and were immediately put in cars, and the officer that promised to send me to my parents refused to do so. We left here at 1, got to Elmira at 8 in the evening.

July 28 — We were treated very good on the road,

and especially at Goshen, N.Y. The ladies gave us eatables and the men gave us tobacco.

July 29 — There are at present some 3,000 prisoners here. I like this place better than Point Lookout. We are fenced in by a high fence, in, I judge, a 200-acre lot. There is an observatory outside, and some Yankee is making money, as he charges ten cents for every one that wishes to see the rebels.

August — Nothing worth recording this month, except that the fare is the same as at Point Lookout.

September — It is very cold, worse than I have seen it in the South in the dead of winter.

October — We have got the smallpox in prison, and from six to twelve are taken out dead daily. We can buy from prisoners rats, 25 cents each, killed and dressed. Quite a number of our boys have gone into the rat business. On the 11th of this month there were 800 sick prisoners sent South on parole.

November and December — Nothing, only bitter cold. We dance every night at some of our quarters. Some of the men put a white handkerchief around one of their arms, and these act as the ladies. We have a jolly good time.

CHAPTER FOUR
The Year 1865

January — Nothing, only that I fear that our cause is lost, as we are losing heavily, and have no more men at home to come to the army. Our resources in everything are at an end, while the enemy are seemingly stronger than ever. All the prisoners in Northern prisons, it seems, will have to stay until the end of the war, as Grant would rather feed than fight us.

February — The smallpox is frightful. There is not a day that at least twenty men are taken out dead. Cold is no name for the weather now. They have given most of us Yankee overcoats, but have cut the skirts off. The reason of this is that the skirts are long and if they left them on we might pass out as Yankee soldiers.

March — Nothing new. It is the same gloomy and discouraging news from the South, and gloomy and discouraging in prison.

April — I suppose the end is near, for there is no more hope for the South to gain her independence. On the 10th of this month we were told by an officer that all those who wished to get out of prison by taking the oath of allegiance to the United States could do so in a very few days. There was quite a consultation among the prisoners. On the morning of the 12th we heard that Lee had surrendered on the 9th, and about 400, myself with them, took the cursed oath and were given transportation to wherever we wanted to go. I took mine to New York City to my parents, whom I have not seen since 1858. Our cause is lost; our comrades who have given their lives for the independence of the South have died in vain; that is, the cause for which they gave their lives is lost, but they positively did not give their lives in vain. They gave it for a most righteous cause, even if the Cause was lost. Those that remain to see the end for which they fought — what have we left? Our sufferings and privations would be nothing had the end been otherwise, for we have suffered hunger, been without sufficient clothing, barefooted, lousy, and have suffered more than any one can believe, except soldiers of the Southern Confederacy. And the end of all is a desolated home to go to. When I commenced this diary of my life as a Confederate soldier I was full of hope for the speedy termination of the war, and our independence. I was not quite nineteen years old. I am now twenty-three. The four years that I have given to my country I do not regret, nor am I sorry for one day that I have given — my only regret is that we have lost that for which we fought. Nor do I for one moment think that we lost it by any other way than by being outnumbered at least five if not ten to one. The world was open to the enemy, but shut out to us. I shall now close this diary in sorrow, but to the last I will say that, although but a private, I still say our Cause was just, nor do I regret one thing that I have done to cripple the North.

The following sketch is taken from Clark's "History of the War," written by my Colonel Morehead. This gives the endurance of my company, regiment and brigade after I was captured.

CHAPTER FIVE
History of the Fifty-Third Regiment
From May 5, 1864

On the 5th or 6th of May, 1864, the sharpshooters of this regiment were much annoyed by one of the Federal sharpshooters, who had a long-range rifle and who had climbed up a tall tree from which he could pick off our men, though sheltered by stump and stones, himself out of range of our guns. Private Leon, of Company B (Mecklenburg), concluded that this thing would have to stop, and taking advantage of every knoll, hollow, and stump, he crawled near enough for his rifle to reach, took a pop at this disturber of the peace, and he came tumbling down. Upon running up to his victim, Leon discovered him to be a Canadian Indian, and clutching his scalp-lock, dragged him to our line of sharpshooters.

The regiment was at Lynchburg when the pursuit of Hunter began. Marching with General Early to Washington, D.C., was one of the regiments left to support the picket line under the walls of Washington, while the rest of the corps made good its retreat to the valley — the Nineteenth and Sixth Corps of the Federal army having been poured into the city for its defense. While supporting the pickets, this regiment became involved in one of the hottest conflicts in its experience, but succeeded in holding its position, repulsing and driving the enemy back to the earthworks which defended the city. At midnight it received orders to retire in perfect silence, and to the surprise of all, when we reached the position on the hills near the city, where we had left the corps, it was ascertained that the corps had left the night before, twenty-four hours — and we marched the whole night and the greater part of the next day before we caught up with the rear guards. Early's ruse, as usual, had succeeded in deceiving the enemy.

This regiment participated in all the battles in the Valley in 1864, and in numerous combats and skirmishes. In this Valley campaign the regiment lost its gallant Colonel Owens, who died at Snicker's Ford, near Snicker's Gap, in August, 1864. He had been absent since the 10th of May, disabled by wounds at Spottsylvania Court House; had returned just as the regiment was eating dinner, and almost while we were congratulating him on his safe return we received notice that the enemy had crossed the river at Snicker's Ford. The order to "fall in" was given, we marched to the river, and drove the enemy across, after a short but severe conflict. The firing had ceased, excepting now and then a dropping shot, when Colonel Owens was killed by one of these stray shots. He was a good officer, brave, humane, social, popular with both men and officers. He was succeeded by the writer as Colonel. At Winchester, on 19th September, 1864, Adjutant Osborne was killed. Two years ago, Color Sergeant

Taylor, of Company E, Surry County, who had resided in Utah since 1866, visited me. He received a ball in his hip, from which wound he still limps, and in talking about his own wound, he told me as we were charging the third Federal line at Winchester, having broken the first two, and when near the temporary breastwork of the enemy he received the shot which disabled him for life, and that, as he fell, young Osborne picked up the flag, and waving it, ran forward, cheering on the men, and was killed within twenty feet of the color sergeant. He was an efficient officer and daring soldier, I suppose not older than twenty years. Lieut. W. R. Murray, of Company A, than whom there was not a better officer or braver soldier in the "Old Guard" of Napoleon, acted as adjutant after the death of Osborne till the surrender of Appomattox.

As stated before, Major Iredell, a true gentleman and brave soldier, was killed at Spottsylvania Court House. Capt. John W. Rierson succeeded him. At Winchester, finding that there was a gap of two or three hundred yards between my left and the troops on the left, and that the enemy had discovered and were preparing to take advantage of it, I directed Major Rierson to find General Grimes on the right of the division (General Rodes had been killed in the beginning of the action), and apprise him of the situation. After some time he returned, saluted, and reported, the fighting being very heavy all the time, when I discovered that Major Rierson was shot through the neck, which wound was received before he found General Grimes, but he nevertheless performed the duty, returned, and reported, and did not then go to the rear until I directed him to do so. This gallant officer was killed when the enemy broke over our lines at Petersburg, a few days before Appomattox. He was entitled to his commission as lieutenant-colonel from the date of the battle of Snicker's Ford, but I do not know that he received it.

This was a volunteer regiment, enlisted in the latter part of the winter and first part of the spring of 1862, and was organized at Camp Mangum, near Raleigh, the first week in May, 1862, and assigned to Daniels' Brigade (Rodes' Division). William A. Owens, of Mecklenburg County, was elected colonel; James T. Morehead, of Guilford County, lieutenant-colonel, and James Johnson Iredell, of Wake County, major.

Colonel Owens had already been in service more than one year, having served as captain in the First (Bethel) Regiment, and at the time of his election was lieutenant-colonel of the Eleventh Regiment.

Lieutenant-Colonel Morehead had also been in the service the year before, having entered the same in April, 1861, as lieutenant of the "Guilford Grays" (afterward Company B of the Twenty-seventh Regiment), and at the time of his election was a captain in the Forty-fifth Regiment.

William B. Osborne, of Mecklenburg County, was appointed captain and assistant quartermaster. He resigned in the fall of 1862, and was succeeded by Capt. John B. Burwell. J.F. Long was appointed surgeon; Lauriston H. Hill, of Stokes County, assistant surgeon, and promoted surgeon in 1863. William Hill, of Mecklenburg, was appointed Captain A.C.S. In 1863, Charles Gresham, of Virginia, was assigned to duty with this regiment as assistant surgeon. James H. Colton, of Randolph County, was appointed chaplain; J.H. Owens, sergeant-major (promoted second lieutenant of Company I and killed); R.B. Burwell, quartermaster-sergeant; J.C. Palmer, commissary sergeant; R.S. Barnett, ordinance sergeant. Upon the promotion of

J.H. Owens, Aaron Katz, of Company B, succeeded him as sergeant-major, and upon his being captured, Robert A. Fleming, of Company A, was sergeant-major.

Company A was from Guilford County. A. P. McDaniel was its first captain, commissioned February 25, 1862, and upon his retirement in 1863, Lieut. J.M. Sutton was promoted captain and wounded at Bethesda Church, and on September 21, 1864, in the Valley, and captured at Petersburg; P. W. Haterick (killed at Gettysburg), first lieutenant; J.M. Sutton, second lieutenant; W.L. Flemming, promoted from sergeant to second lieutenant in 1863; J.W. Scott, promoted second lieutenant from sergeant (chief of regimental corps of sharpshooters).

Company B was from Mecklenburg County, and its first captain was J. Harvey White, commissioned March 1, 1862, killed at Spottsylvania Court House in May, 1864. Samuel E. Belk, first lieutenant; John M. Springs, second lieutenant, promoted assistant quartermaster; William M. Matthews, second lieutenant, promoted from first sergeant; M. E. Alexander, promoted second lieutenant from second sergeant. Lieutenants Belk, Matthews and Alexander were wounded at Gettysburg.

Company C was from Johnston, Chatham, and Wake, mostly from Johnston. Its first captain was John Leach, commissioned February 28, 1862; was succeeded as captain by J.C. Richardson (wounded at Petersburg), commissioned April 27, 1863, both from Johnston County; George T. Leach, of Chatham, commissioned first lieutenant March 7, 1862; John H. Tomlinson, of Johnston County, commissioned second lieutenant July 21, 1862.

Company D was from Guilford, Cumberland, Forsyth, Stokes, Bladen, and Surry. David Scott, Jr., of Guilford County, was commissioned captain March 1, 1862, resigned, and was succeeded May 15, 1863, by Alexander Ray, of Cumberland County, promoted from first lieutenant and killed at Petersburg, April, 1865. Alexander Ray was commissioned first lieutenant March 1, 1862; Madison L. Efland, of Guilford County, commissioned second lieutenant March 1, 1862, promoted first lieutenant May 15, 1863, and wounded; A. H. Westmoreland, Stokes County, was promoted from the ranks to second lieutenant in 1863.

Company E was from Surry County. J.C. Norman was commissioned captain on March 8, 1862, resigned the following December, and was succeeded by First Lieut. Rogert A. Hill, killed in 1864, succeeded in turn as captain by First Lieut. B.W. Minter; Samuel Walker was commissioned second lieutenant March 8, 1862, promoted to first lieutenant December, 1862, and resigned; B.W. Minter, second lieutenant, promoted first lieutenant and captain; Henry Hines, second lieutenant, in 1862; Logan Bemer, promoted from corporal to second lieutenant, wounded and captured, in 1864; James A. Hill, second lieutenant, captured in 1864.

Company F was from Alamance and Chatham. G. M.G. Albright was commissioned captain May 5, 1862, killed July, 1863, at Gettysburg, and succeeded by A.G. Albright, promoted from first lieutenant (wounded at Fisher's Hill, 1864); Jesse M. Holt, first lieutenant, July 16, 1863, promoted from second lieutenant (killed at Winchester, 1864); Branson Lambe, commissioned in 1864, promoted from second lieutenant; John J. Webster, commissioned second lieutenant May, 1862, and resigned; S. J. Albright, commissioned second lieutenant in 1862, and killed at Spottsylvania Court House in 1864.

Company G was from Stokes County. Capt. Spottswood B. Taylor was commissioned captain on March 20, 1862, and resigned May, 1862; was succeeded by John W. Rierson, promoted from second lieutenant, and who was, in 1863, promoted to major, wounded at Winchester, and killed at Petersburg, April, 1865. He was in time succeeded as captain by H.H. Campbell, promoted from first lieutenant, and killed at Winchester. G. B. Moore was commissioned first lieutenant in March, 1862, and resigned in June; John W. Rierson commissioned second lieutenant March, 1862; W.H. McKinney was promoted from the ranks in May, 1862, to second lieutenant, and wounded at Winchester; C. F. Hall, promoted from the ranks to second lieutenant, mortally wounded at Gettysburg; W. F. Campbell, promoted first lieutenant, and wounded at Washington, D.C.

Company H was from Stokes County. Capt. Spottswood B. Taylor was commissioned on March 20, 1862, and resigned on account of ill-health, November, 1863, and was succeeded by John E. Miller, promoted from second lieutenant, who was wounded at Snicker's Ford and captured, 1864; Thomas S. Burnett, commissioned first lieutenant March 20, 1862, and killed in 1863; Charles A. McGehee, first lieutenant, 1862, wounded at Gettysburg, July, 1863, and captured; Alexander M. King, second lieutenant, March, 1862; J. Henry Owens, promoted second lieutenant from sergeant-major, December, 1862, and killed; Alexander Boyles, promoted first lieutenant.

Company I was from Union County. E.A. Jerome was commissioned captain March 20, 1862, and resigned in June following, and was succeeded by Thomas E. Ashcraft, promoted from first lieutenant; John D. Cuthbertson, commissioned second lieutenant March 20, 1862, promoted first lieutenant; Joshua Lee, commissioned second lieutenant March 20, 1862; James E. Green, promoted from the ranks, second lieutenant, June 24, 1862; A. T. Marsh, promoted from sergeant to second lieutenant May 19, 1864. Company K was from Wilkes County. William J. Miller was commissioned captain March 20, 1862, killed at Gettysburg, July 1, 1863, and was succeeded by Jesse F. Eller, promoted from second lieutenant; Thomas C. Miller, promoted from second lieutenant to first lieutenant, July 1, 1863; Thomas C. Miller, commissioned to second lieutenant in August, 1862.

This regiment lost in killed its first colonel, who was twice wounded; both of its majors, one of them, Rierson, several times wounded, and its adjutant. Its surviving colonel was wounded three times — at Gettysburg, Fisher's Hill, and in the assault upon the Federal lines at Hare's Hill on March 25, 1865, in which last engagement he was captured within the enemy's works.

As it is, I have only the approximately correct report of the losses of one of the companies of the regiment, and that only in one battle, but I think the losses of the other companies may be fairly estimated from the losses of this one.

Company B lost at Gettysburg, out of sixty-five men, eight killed and twenty-two wounded, and of the four officers, three were wounded.

I meet many of these scarred and now grizzly veterans of the companies from Alamance, Guilford, Stokes, and Surry at my courts in these counties, and hear, sometimes from those from the other counties, and with very few exceptions, they have shown themselves to be as good citizens as they were gallant soldiers. They illustrate that "peace hath her victories no less renowned than war."

The regiment, reduced to a handful of men, shared the fortunes of the historic retreat, and surrendered at Appomattox, being then commanded by Capt. Thomas E. Ashcraft, the brigade being commanded by Col. David G. Cowand. General Grimes having been made a major-general, commanded the division.

I cannot close this sketch without acknowledging my indebtedness to Captain Sutton and Private J. Montgomery, of Company A; L. Leon, of Company B, who kindly furnished me with copy of a diary kept by him from the organization of the regiment up to May, 1864, when he was captured; Captain Albright, of Company F; Capt. S.B. Taylor, of Company H, and Lieut. W.F. Campbell, of Company G, for valuable information; and the hope that the publication of the sketches of the North Carolina regiments will excite interest enough among the old soldiers to give us further dates and incidents. I wish I could write a history of my regiment which would do the officers and men full credit for their patriotism and services.

The patriotism and heroism of these soldiers were illustrated by the patient and uncomplaining endurance of the forced march, the short rations, the hardships of winter camps and campaigns as much as by their fighting qualities. Posterity will hesitate to decide which is most worthy of admiration.

James T. Morehead
Greensboro, N.C.,
April 9, 1901.

FIRST NORTH CAROLINA REGIMENT

Roster of Companies

Co. A. Edgecombe Guards. Capt. John L. Bridgers.
Co. B. Hornet's Nest Riflemen. Capt. L.S. Williams.
Co. C. Charlotte Grays. Capt. E.A. Ross.
Co. D. Orange Light Infantry. Capt. R.J. Ashe.
Co. E. Buncombe Riflemen. Capt. W.W. McDowell.
Co. F. Lafayette Light Infantry. Capt. J.B. Starr.
Co. G. Burke Rifles. Capt. C.N. Avery.
Co. H. Fayetteville Independent Light Infantry. Capt. W.
Huske.
Co. I. Enfield Blues. Capt. D.B. Bell.
Co. K. Southern Stars. Capt. W.J. Hoke.

ROLL OF CHARLOTTE GRAYS.
COMPANY C, FIRST N.C.
BETHEL REGIMENT

Enlisted April, 1861

E.A. Ross, Capt., P. Maj. of 11th N.C.
E.B. Cohen, 1st lieut.
T.B. Trotter, 2nd lieut.
C.W. Alexander, 2nd lieut.
C.R. Staley, orderly sergeant.
J.P. Elms, 2nd sergeant, P. lieut., 37th N.C.
J.G. McCorkle, 3rd lieut.
W.G. Berryhill, 4th lieut.
D.L. Bringle, 5th or Ensign.
W.D. Elms, 1st corporal, P. Capt., 37th N.C.
W.B. Taylor, 2nd corporal, P. 2nd liet., Co. A, 11th N.C.
Henry Terris, 3rd corporal.
George Wolfe, 4th corporal.
Dr. J.B. Boyd, surgeon.

Privates

M.R. Alexander.
T.A. Alexander.
Lindsey Adams.
J. P. Andrey, P. Capt., 49th N.C.
W.E. Andrey, P. Capt., 30th N.C.
A.H. Brown.
Wm. Brown.
Wm. J. Brown.
Ed. F. Britton.
L. Behrends.
Wm. Calder.
J.W. Cathey.
S.P. Caldwell.
J.F. Crawson.
T.B. Cowan.
T.J. Campbell.
J.W. Clendennen.
J.F. Collins.
T.G. Davis.
J. T. Downs, P. Lieut., 30th N.C.
L.W. Downs.
J.P.A. Davidson.
J.R. Dunn.
J. Engel.
J.M. Earnheanut.
M.F. Ezzell.
J.A. Ezzell.
S.H. Elliott.
J.A. Elliott.
R.H. Flow.
James Flore.

I.S.A. Frazier.
R.H. Grier, P.Lieut., 49th N.C.
J.C. Grier, P. Capt., 49th N.C.
J.M. Grier.
J.A. Gibson.
D.P. Glenn.
J.R. Gribble.
N. Gray.
R.L. Gillespie.
D.W. Hall.
J.C. Hill.
W.J. Hill.
H.H. Hill.
W. Lee Harrel, P. Capt., A 11th N.C.
Robt. H. Hand, P. Lieut., A 11th N.C.
R.H. Howard.
Thomas Howard.
Jas. M. Hutchison.
Cynes N. Hutchison.
Tom F. Hoton.
Tom H. Harkey.
S. Hymans.
Harper C. Houston.
T. Lindsey Holms.
Jas. T. Haskell.
W.T. Hanser.
George T. Herron.
Geo. W. Howey.
Jacob Harkey.
L.P. Henderson.
Jack R. Isreal.
Wm. S. Icehower.

E.P. Ingold.
Robt. W. Johnston.
Jacob Katz.
Wm. H. Kistler.
Jack A. Kinsey.
J.H. Knox.
Robt. Keenan.
Louis Leon.
J.C. Levi.
Jacob Leopold.
Henry Moyle.
Tom F. McGinn.
John McKinley.
Wm. McKeever.
D. Watt McDonald.
John H. McDonald.
Robt. J. Monteith.
Moses O. Monteith.
Sam'l J. McElroy.
Jack Norment.
Isaac Norment.
Wm. B. Neal.
L.M. Neal.
S.R. Neal.
P.A. Neal.
Thos. W. Neely.
S. Oppenheim.
J.T. Orr.
John L. Osborne.
J.E. Orman.
Mack Pettus.
S.A. Phillips.
W.R. Carter.
R.A. Carter.
John G. Cotts, P. Lieut., 49th
        Rgt.

Wm. M. Patts.
Lawson A. Cotts, P. Capt.,
        37th N.C.
Calvin M. Queny.
Theo. C. Ruddock.
J.R. Rea.
D.B. Rea.
Wm. D. Stone.
W. Steele.
Jim W. Stowe.
Wm. E. Sizer.
J. Monroe Sims, Q.M. Sergt.,
        11th N.C.
Richard A. Springs.
C. Ed. Smith.
S.B. Smith.
M.H. Smith.
W.J.B. Smith.
W.H. Saville.
John W. Sample.
David I. Sample.
James M. Saville.
Robt. Frank Simpson.
S.E. Todd.
Wm. Todd.
John W. Treloan.
Hugh A. Tate.
Charles B. Watt.
B. Frank Watt.
C.C. Wingate.
T.D. Wolfe.
T.J. Wolfe.
John Wiley.

Total, 143 officers and men.

FIFTY-THIRD NORTH CAROLINA REGIMENT

Roster of Companies

Co. A. Guilford. Capt. A.P. McDaniel.
Co. B. Mecklenberg. Capt. J.H. White.
Co. C. Johnson; Chatham; Wake. Capt. John Leach.
Co. D. Guilford; Cumberland; Forsythe; Stokes;
    Bladen; Surry. Capt. David Scott.
Co. E. Surry. Capt. J.C. Norman.
Co. F. Alamance; Chatham. Capt. G.M.G. Albright.
Co. G. Stokes. Capt. G.W. Clark.
Co. H. Stokes. Capt. S.B. Taylor.
Co. I. Union. Capt. Thomas E. Ashcraft.
Co. K. Wilkes. Capt. W.J. Miller.

COMPANY B, 53RD REGIMENT, N.C.T., C.S.A. FROM MECKLENBURG

J.H. White, captain, k.   W.M. Matthews, lieut.
S.E. Belk, captain, k.   M.E. Alexander, lieut.
J.M. Springs, lieut.

Non-Commissioned Officers

R.J. Patterson, w.   W.R. Baily.
S.M. Blair.   R.H. Todd, k.
R.A. Davis.   W.H. Alexander, k.
A.N. Gray.

Privates

Alexander, J.W., d.
Alexander, Benj. P., d.
Alexander, Benj. C.
Anderson, Wm., d.
Atchison, Wm., c. and w.
Armstrong, Leroy, c.
Barnett, W.A., k.
Barnett, R.S.
Barnett E.L.S.
Berryhill, W.A., c.
Berryhill, Andrew, w.
Berryhill, Alex.
Barnes, S.S., d.
Bruce, G.W.
Burwell, J.B.
Benton, Sam'l, w.
Cochran, J.M.
Cochran, Wm. R.
Cochran, R.C.
Catchcoat, J.H., w.
Capps, John, d.
Caton, Elijah, w. and c.
Caton, Sylv., c. and d.
Clark, W.H.
Clark, W.C.
Clark, A.W.
Collins, John, k.
Campbell, J.P.
Davis, W.A., d.
Demon, Jacob.
Donnell, W.T., w. and c.
Engenburn, John, w.
Eagle, W.H.
Epps, W.D., k.

Engel, Jonas.
Frazier, J.L.
Fincher, Asa.
Farrices, Z.W.
Frazier, J.C.R.
Grier, J.G., w.
Giles, M.O.
Giles, S.H.
Howie, J.M.
Howie, Sam'l M., w.
Howie, F.M., w.
Hall, H.L., w.
Hood, R.L., c.
Harry, W.B., w.
Hoover, F.M.
Katz, Aaron.
King, P.A., k.
Kirkpatrick, T.A.
Knox, J.S.
Leon, Louis.
Love, D.L.
Marks, S.S., c.
Marks, J.G., w.
Marks, T.E., k.
Marks, W.S.
McGinn, Thos.
McElroy, Jas. W., k.
Mitchell, C.J.
McKinney, Wm.
McKinney, T.A., c.
Merritt, Wm. N., k.
McCrary, Jordan.
Morrison, J.M.
McCombs, A.H., w. and c.

Maxwell, P.P., w.
McCrum, H.A., k.
Norment, A.A., k.
Otters, Cooney, c. and d.
Owens, J. Henry, k.
Oates, Jas.
Potts, Jas. H.
Patterson, S.L.
Parks, Miah, c.
Reid, H.K.
Reid, J.F., k.
Robinson, Thomp.
Russell, H.T., c.
Rodden, N.B., w.
Rodden, W.R., k.
Robinson, J.P.
Smith, Lemuel.
Sweat, J.M.
Sample, H.B., c.
Sample, David.
Sample, J.W.
Sample, J.M., c.
Springs, R.A.
Stone, W.D., w. and c.
Sulivan, W.L.

Stewart, W.S., d.
Taylor, J.W., w.
Todd, S.E.
Thomas, Henry.
Trotter, A.G.
Trotter, Thos., d.
Vickers, E.N.
Worthern, Henry, d.
Wilkenson, Neil, k.
Wolfe, C.H.
Winders, P.S., c.
Wilson, L.R., c.
Wilson, J.H., k.
Wilson, S.W., w. and c.
Wilson, J.M.
Wilkinson, R.L.
Williams, Hugh.
Williams, J.W.
Williams, A.L.
Williamson, A.L., c.
Williamson, J.M., c.
White, J.T.

Total, 110; killed, 16; wounded 21; died, 12; captured, 20.

Made in the USA
Columbia, SC
25 October 2021